The Awe of God

THE ASTOUNDING WAY A HEALTHY FEAR OF GOD TRANSFORMS YOUR LIFE

BIBLE STUDY GUIDE

JOHN BEVERE

HarperChristian Resources

The Awe of God Bible Study Guide
© 2023 by John Bevere

Requests for information should be addressed to:
HarperChristian Resources, 3900 Sparks Dr. SE, Grand Rapids, Michigan 49546

ISBN 978-0-310-16335-0 (softcover)
ISBN 978-0-310-16336-7 (ebook)

HarperChristian Resources titles may be purchased in bulk for church, business, fundraising, or ministry use. For information, please e-mail ResourceSpecialist@ChurchSource.com.

Published in association with the Fedd Agency, www.thefeddagency.com.

Printed in the United States of America

24 25 26 27 28 LBC 12 11 10 9 8

CONTENTS

The words of the wise are like cattle prods—

painful but helpful.

Their collected sayings are like a nail-studded stick

with which a shepherd drives the sheep.

But, my child, let me give you some further advice:

Be careful, for writing books is endless,

and much study wears you out.

That's the whole story.

Here now is my final conclusion:

Fear God and obey his commands,

for this is everyone's duty.

God will judge us for everything we do,

including every secret thing, whether good or bad.

ECCLESIASTES 12:11-14 NLT

HOW TO USE THIS GUIDE

The Bible tells us—about 365 times—to "fear not." This leads many Christians to conclude that God does not want us ever to fear. But all these verses refer to *destructive fear*. There are around 200 other verses that encourage us to "fear God." Here is the unfortunate reality for many of us. In our quest to eliminate all *destructive* fears, we have also thrown out a *healthy* fear extolled throughout Scripture: *the fear of the Lord*.

This is the purpose of this study. During the next six weeks, you will explore how rightly directed fear—specifically the biblical virtue of fearing God above anything else in this life—will open up the path to a life that is greater than anything you have ever imagined. You will also see that the fear of the Lord will draw you into great intimacy with your Creator and enable you to confront and overcome anything that this life throws at you.

Now, before you begin, keep in mind that there are a few ways you can go through this material. You can experience this study with others in a group (such as a Bible study, Sunday school class, or any other small-group gathering), or you may choose to go through the content on your own. Either way, know that the videos for each session are available for you to view at any time by following the instructions provided on the inside cover of this study guide.

GROUP STUDY

Each of the sessions in this study are divided into two parts: (1) a group study section, and (2) a personal study section. The group study section provides a basic framework on how to open your time together, get the most out of the video content, and discuss the key ideas that were presented in the teaching. Each session includes the following:

- **Welcome:** A short note about the topic of the session for you to read on your own before you meet as a group.
- **Connect:** A few icebreaker questions to get you and your group members thinking about the topic and interacting with each other.
- **Watch:** An outline of the key points covered in each video teaching along with space for you to take notes as you watch each session.

- **Discuss:** Questions to help you and your group reflect on the teaching material presented and apply it to your lives.
- **Respond:** A short personal exercise to help reinforce the key ideas.
- **Pray:** A place for you to record prayer requests and praises for the week.

If you are doing this study with a group, make sure that you have your own copy of the study guide so you can write down your thoughts, responses, insights, and reflections each week—and so you have access to all the videos via streaming. You will also want to have a copy of *The Awe of God* book, as reading it alongside the curriculum will provide you with deeper insights. (See the notes at the beginning of each group session and personal study section on which chapters of the book you should read before the next group session.)

Finally, keep these points in mind:

- **Facilitation:** If you are doing this study in a group, you will want to appoint someone to serve as a facilitator. This person will be responsible for starting the video and keeping track of time during discussions and activities. If *you* have been chosen for this role, there are some resources in the back of this guide that can help you lead your group through the study.

- **Faithfulness:** Your group is a place where tremendous growth can happen as you reflect on the Bible, ask questions, and learn what God is doing in other people's lives. For this reason, be fully committed and attend each session so you can build trust and rapport with the other members.

- **Friendship:** The goal of any small group is to serve as a place where people can share, learn about God, and build friendships. So make your group a "safe place." Be honest about your thoughts and feelings, but also listen carefully to everyone else's thoughts, feelings, and opinions. Keep anything personal that your group members share in confidence so that you can create a community where people can heal, be challenged, and grow spiritually.

If you are going through this study on your own, read the opening Welcome section and reflect on the questions in the Connect section. Watch the video and use the prompts that have been provided to take notes. Finally, personalize the questions and exercises in the Discuss and Respond sections. Close by recording any requests that you want to pray about during the week.

PERSONAL STUDY

The personal study is for you to go work through on your own during the week. Each exercise is designed to help you explore the key ideas you uncovered during your group time and delve into passages of Scripture that will help you apply those principles to your life. Go at your own pace, doing a little each day—or tackle the material all at once. Remember to spend a few moments in silence to listen to whatever God might be saying to you.

Note that if you are doing this study as part of a group, and you are unable to finish (or even start) these personal studies for the week, you should still attend the group time. Be assured that you are still wanted and welcome even if you don't have your "homework" done. The group studies and personal studies are intended to help you hear what God wants you to hear and how to apply what he is saying to your life. So . . . as you go through this study, be listening for him to speak to you as you learn about the holy fear of God.

WEEK 1

BEFORE GROUP MEETING	Read the Introduction and chapters 1–7 in *The Awe of God* Read the Welcome section (page 3)
GROUP MEETING	Discuss the Connect questions Watch the video teaching for session 1 Discuss the questions that follow as a group Do the closing exercise and pray (pages 3–8)
STUDY 1	Complete the personal study (pages 10–12)
STUDY 2	Complete the personal study (pages 13–15)
STUDY 3	Complete the personal study (pages 16–17)
CONNECT & DISCUSS	Connect with someone in your group (page 18)
CATCH UP & READ AHEAD (before week 2 group meeting)	Read chapters 8–14 in *The Awe of God* Complete any unfinished personal studies (page 19)

HOLY
AWE

The fear of the Lord is the beginning of knowledge,
but fools despise wisdom and instruction.

PROVERBS 1:7

The **remark able** thing about *fearing God* **is that when you fear God you fear nothing else, whereas** *if you do not fear God* **you fear everything else.**

OSWALD CHAMBERS[1]

Fear, **when rightly employed, is the very brightest state of Christianity. . . .** *"The fear of God"* **is the constant description which the Scripture gives of** *true religion*.

CHARLES SPURGEON[2]

WELCOME | READ ON YOUR OWN

Many of us today believe that certain emotions are always wrong, always destructive, and always inappropriate. Like hatred, for example. We're often told followers of Jesus should be creatures of love, not hate. After all, the Bible says God is love, and because hatred is the opposite of love, hatred must be inherently immoral. It's common to hear similar sentiments about other feelings—jealousy, rage, despair, and so on.

But wait a minute. Let's take a moment to assess those assumptions. In Proverbs, we read "there are six things the Lord hates" (see 6:16–19). So God experiences hatred. Scripture also says God is jealous (see Exodus 20:5), that God's fierce anger "raged against the towns of Judah" (Jeremiah 44:6), and that Jesus, "being in anguish," prayed so intensely His sweat was like drops of blood (see Luke 22:44).

In short, God experiences hatred, jealousy, rage, and despair. Now, this is not to say that God's people should act in a hateful, jealous, or enraged manner. It is simply to say that we need to recalibrate our thoughts when it comes to negative emotions, because it's not necessarily the emotions themselves that are dangerous. What *is* dangerous is choosing to think, feel, or act in ways that conflict with how God thinks, feels, and acts.

As we will see in this session, fear is another emotion that can use some recalibration in the church. Many of us have been taught that fear is always negative—always something to be avoided. In reality, fear is an essential element of life. This is especially true when we consider what the Bible says about the fear of the Lord.

CONNECT | 15 MINUTES

If any of your group members don't know each other, take a few minutes to introduce yourselves. Then, to get things started, discuss one of the following questions:

- Why did you decide to join this study? What do you hope to learn?

  — *or* —

- On a scale of 1 (rarely) to 10 (regularly), how often do you experience the emotion of fear?

WATCH | 20 MINUTES

Now watch the video for this session, which you can access by playing the DVD or through streaming (see the instructions provided on the inside front cover). Below is an outline of the key points covered during the teaching. Record any key concepts that stand out to you on the following page.

OUTLINE

I. There is a hidden virtue that, in essence, is the key to all of life.
   A. This secret virtue offers the essential ingredient for being close with God.
   B. This virtue can help safeguard your faith and the faith of your loved ones.
   C. This virtue can help you remove behaviors that harm you spiritually.

II. This secret virtue is the fear of God.
   A. King Solomon, one of the wisest men to ever live, wrote about this virtue.
   B. Solomon was trained in the fear of God and his success as king was largely based on that virtue.
   C. Solomon lost sight of this virtue toward the end of his life but didn't die in that state.

III. There is a difference between the fear of the Lord and being scared of God.
   A. There are harmful fears . . . but there are also healthy fears.
   B. The person who is scared of God has something to hide.
   C. The fear of God is not being afraid of God but being afraid of being away from Him.

IV. The fear of the Lord includes more than just reverence.
   A. The fear of God does include esteem, respect, honor, and veneration.
   B. To fear God also means to give Him all that belongs to Him.

V. The key benefits to fearing God.
   A. The fear of God increases our intimacy with Him.
   B. The fear of God is the beginning of wisdom, knowledge, and understanding.
   C. The fear of God provides the pathway for us to mature in our salvation.
   D. The fear of God produces authentic holiness.
   E. The fear of God swallows up all other fears, including the fear of man.

NOTES

DISCUSS | 35 MINUTES

Take time to discuss what you just watched by answering the following questions.

1. The "fear of God" is one of those terms that gets used a lot in church settings but is rarely defined. In your own words, how would you summarize what you've been taught about "the fear of God"? What does it mean? What does it *not* mean?

2. At the end of the book of Ecclesiastes, Solomon sums up the wisdom of his experience by saying, "Fear God and keep his commandments, for this is the duty of all mankind" (12:13). How would you describe the connection between fearing God and obeying God?

3. Look again at Hebrews 12:28–29: "Therefore, since we are receiving a kingdom that cannot be shaken, let us be thankful, and so worship God acceptably with reverence and awe, for our 'God is a consuming fire.'" How does the fear of God lead to worship, and vice versa?

4. The key idea in this study is that holy fear—what we might call the awe of God—is an incredibly powerful force for good in our lives. When have you experienced benefit or blessing because you chose to fear God?

5. Think back to your first encounters with God and your earliest memories of meeting Him. What emotions were most prominent in those encounters? What thoughts or feelings were most prevalent in those experiences?

RESPOND | 10 MINUTES

When God rescued His people from slavery in Egypt, He did not immediately lead them into the promised land. Instead, He led them to Mount Sinai so they could experience Him. Take a few minutes on your own to read about this encounter and then answer the questions that follow.

> [16] On the morning of the third day there was thunder and lightning, with a thick cloud over the mountain, and a very loud trumpet blast. Everyone in the camp trembled. [17] Then Moses led the people out of the camp to meet with God, and they stood at the foot of the mountain. [18] Mount Sinai was covered with smoke, because the LORD descended on it in fire. The smoke billowed up from it like smoke from a furnace, and the whole mountain trembled violently. [19] As the sound of the trumpet grew louder and louder, Moses spoke and the voice of God answered him.
>
> EXODUS 19:16–19

> [18] When the people saw the thunder and lightning and heard the trumpet and saw the mountain in smoke, they trembled with fear. They stayed at a distance [19] and said to Moses, "Speak to us yourself and we will listen. But do not have God speak to us or we will die." [20] Moses said to the people, "Do not be afraid. God has come to test you, so that the fear of God will be with you to keep you from sinning." [21] The people remained at a distance, while Moses approached the thick darkness where God was.
>
> EXODUS 20:18–21

How do these passages add to your understanding of what it means to fear God?

What are some ways that the fear of God will keep us from sinning?

PRAY | 10 MINUTES

Praying for one another is one of the most important things you can do as a community. So use this time wisely and make it more than just a "closing prayer" to end your group experience. Be intentional about sharing your prayers, reviewing how God is answering your prayers, and actually praying for each other as a group. When you come to a close, express your desire to better understand the fear of God. Ask God to bless you not only with knowledge about that fear, but also with experience. Ask Him to fill every person in your group with holy fear. Afterward, use the space below to write down any requests mentioned so that you and your group members can continue to pray about them in the week ahead.

Name   Request

PERSONAL STUDY

You are on a journey toward a better understanding of what it means to fear the Lord. A key part of that growth, regardless of where you are spiritually, involves studying Scripture. This is the goal of these personal studies—to help you explore what the Bible has to say and how to apply God's Word to your life. As you work through each of these exercises, be sure to write down your responses to the questions, as you will be given a few minutes to share your insights at the start of the next session if you are doing this study with others. If you are reading *The Awe of God* alongside this study, first review the Introduction and chapters 1–7 of the book.

WHAT IS HOLY FEAR?

As we study Scripture, it's important to work through any misunderstandings that have the potential to hold us back. For example, as we discussed earlier, many believe fear is always a bad thing—something that is spiritually harmful. In reality, the fear of God is a foundational element of what it means to live out our calling as disciples of Christ.

There are also some who consider the fear of the Lord to be related to Old-Testament times. They perceive God as a figure of wrath and judgment in the Old Testament, while in the New Testament, He demonstrates love and grace. But even a cursory glance through books such as Genesis, Judges, Isaiah, and Psalms reveal the Old Testament is filled with passages about God's love. Furthermore, you can't read through the Gospels or Revelation without being confronted with the reality of God's judgment and wrath.

The author of Hebrews wrote, "Jesus Christ is the same yesterday and today and forever" (13:8). In other words, the fear of the Lord is not an Old Testament concept or a New Testament concept. It's a *biblical* concept—and one we need to thoroughly understand in order to experience everything God desires for us as His children. So, over the course of this week's personal studies, let's work through what it means to fear God.

1. As you discussed in this week's group time, the fear of the Lord does not mean being *scared* of God so you run from His presence. Rather, the fear of God is a mix of actions and attitudes that draw you *closer* to Him. In fact, fearing the Lord means being terrified of being *apart* from Him. What is one season of your life in which you felt distance or separation between yourself and God? How did that separation affect you?

2. What are some steps you take in your spiritual life to draw near to God? How do you seek out closeness with Him?

It's impossible to define holy fear in a single sentence, paragraph, or chapter. It's no different than attempting to give the full breadth of God's love in the same space. . . . In fact, I believe we'll continue to discover the depths of both holy love and fear throughout eternity. With that said, let me offer a general outline of holy fear's definition. Think back to your childhood when you were given a coloring book and crayons. You opened the book, picked out a page, and found an outline just waiting to be filled in with color. In a similar way, this opening session gives us the borders, but it will take the rest of the study to fill in the colors. If you only go through this session, you'll get a broad idea of holy fear but miss out on its transformational truths.[3]

3. Start to draw the "boundaries" of your definition of holy fear. First, what would you say the fear of God *is not*?

Let's begin by listing our definitions. To fear God is to *reverence* and be in complete *awe* of Him. To fear God is to *hallow* Him. *Hallow* is defined as, "to respect greatly." To fear God is to esteem, respect, honor, venerate, and adore Him above anyone or anything else. When we fear God, we take on His heart. We love what He loves and we hate what He hates. (Notice it is not to "dislike" what He hates, rather it is to "hate" what He hates.) What is important to Him becomes important to us. What is not so important to Him becomes not so important to us.[4]

4. Which of these definitions is most helpful to you in forming your definition of holy fear? Which of these definitions or statements caused you to feel convicted? Why?

5. Reverence for God is part of what it means to fear God. On a practical level, what does it look like for you to esteem, respect, honor, or venerate God above everything else?

GOD'S TANGIBLE PRESENCE

We've made the case in this first session that a genuine fear of the Lord does not drive us away from Him but instead draws us closer to Him. We will keep reiterating this point throughout this study . . . it's that important! The reason we need to keep returning to this point is because each of us needs God's presence in our lives. We were created to live in community with Him. We were designed to be surrounded and uplifted by His Spirit.

Now, this might sound confusing because of what we know about God's nature: *He is omnipresent*. In other words, He exists everywhere. There is no place we can go here on earth (or anywhere else for that matter) that will be removed from God's presence. So, why do we need holy fear to draw us *into* God's presence and increase our connection with Him?

An understanding can be found in the two definitions for God's presence given in Scripture. The first definition relates to God's omnipresence that we've just discussed. The second definition relates to God's presence with His people. In the story of the Exodus, for example, we read the following interaction between God and Moses:

> The LORD replied, "My Presence will go with you, and I will give you rest."
>
> Then Moses said to him, "If your Presence does not go with us, do not send us up from here. How will anyone know that you are pleased with me and with your people unless you go with us? What else will distinguish me and your people from all the other people on the face of the earth?"
>
> And the LORD said to Moses, "I will do the very thing you have asked, because I am pleased with you and I know you by name."
>
> EXODUS 33:14-17

God desires to manifest Himself in the presence of His people—and because of this, we can have a meaning connection with Him. This connection comes when we choose to demonstrate fear of the Lord and draw close in fellowship with Him. As Jesus said about the one who follows Him: "I will love him and manifest Myself to him" (John 14:21 NKJV).

1. When was the last time you felt God's tangible presence in your life in a meaningful way? What caused you to connect with Him at that moment?

2. What spiritual disciplines help you to experience God's presence? If you wanted to spend time in His presence right now, what steps would you take to get there?

The fear of God seems counterintuitive. When hearing the word *fear*, our minds go immediately to a detrimental or even damaging state. But I assure you, it's the greatest force of confidence, comfort, and protection available to any being in the universe. . . . Holy fear can be broken down into two major categories: (1) to *tremble at the presence of God*, and (2) to *tremble at His Word*. . . . Let's begin by highlighting the first. The psalmist declares, "God is *greatly to be feared* in the assembly of the saints, and to be held in *reverence* by all those around Him" (Psalm 89:7 NKJV). Notice it says not merely feared, but rather, "*greatly*" feared. Here's a firm truth: you will never find God's wonderful presence in an atmosphere where He's not revered and held in awe.[5]

3. How would you describe our culture's attitude toward God? Individually, what are some ways we display a lack of reverence for God that pushes us away from His presence?

4. Think about worship. When has the act of worshiping God—either corporately or privately—ushered you into a deeper experience with God's presence and power?

5. Use the following scales to rate the "holy fear factor" in your life. To what degree do you experience holy awe in each of these situations?

How often do you experience holy fear during your personal devotions?

```
O———O———O———O———O———O———O———O———O———O
1    2    3    4    5    6    7    8    9    10
```
[Rarely]   [Regularly]

How often do you experience holy fear at church?

```
O———O———O———O———O———O———O———O———O———O
1    2    3    4    5    6    7    8    9    10
```
[Rarely]   [Regularly]

How often do you experience holy fear while worshiping?

```
O———O———O———O———O———O———O———O———O———O
1    2    3    4    5    6    7    8    9    10
```
[Rarely]   [Regularly]

How often do you experience holy fear in your home?

```
O———O———O———O———O———O———O———O———O———O
1    2    3    4    5    6    7    8    9    10
```
[Rarely]   [Regularly]

THE GLORY OF GOD

In the short history of the United States, there have been many individuals whom we would consider great. People such as George Washington, Harriet Tubman, Abraham Lincoln, Susan B. Anthony, Dr. Martin Luther King Jr., and so on. They are legends.

These individuals are revered in our society. We celebrate holidays in their honor. We carve their images into statues and monuments. We don't speak about them in the same way that we speak about "normal" folks, because their names and their stories carry a special kind of weight that adds substance to their histories.

You could say that such people have acquired a form of glory, and the reality of that glory changes the ways in which we relate to them as individuals and as a culture. Something similar happens in terms of our relationship with God—except on a grander scale. The more we begin to understand how incomparably great and overwhelmingly awesome God is, the more we will experience holy fear in all of our dealings with Him.

God's glory creates a weight that draws us deeper and deeper into His presence.

1. In your own words, how would you describe the concept of God's "glory"? What is it, and why is it important?

What was Isaiah's response in beholding the Lord's glory? It wasn't, "Wow, there He is!" No, he cried out, "It's all over! I'm doomed, for I am a sinful man. I have filthy lips" (Isaiah 6:5 NLT). . . .

How about Job? The Almighty says about him, "'Have you noticed my servant Job? He is the finest man in all the earth'" (Job 1:8 NLT). Can you imagine God saying this about you or me? We would be jumping up and down with joy! Yet, this man encounters God's glory and cries out, "'I have heard of You by the hearing of the ear, but now my eye sees You. Therefore I abhor myself'" (Job 42:5–6 NKJV).

How about Ezekiel? He saw the Lord and wrote, "This is what the glory of the LORD looked like to me. When I saw it, I fell face down on the ground" (Ezekiel 1:28 NLT).

Or what about Abraham? We read that when he saw God, "Abram fell face down on the ground" (Genesis 17:3 NLT).

When God gloriously manifested on Sinai, we read, "Moses himself was so frightened at the sight that he said, 'I am terrified and trembling'" (Hebrews 12:21 NLT).

John the Apostle, the one Jesus loved, writes of his encounter with our glorified Jesus, "When I saw him, I fell at his feet as if I were dead" (Revelation 1:17 NLT).[6]

2. How do the above verses contribute to your understanding of "the fear of God"? When has the Holy Spirit produced this kind of conviction in your heart and mind?

3. Our culture does not have a problem with recognizing glory and responding with worship. The problem is that we revere the glory of *human beings* rather than God. Where do you see examples of this in the world today? How have you been guilty of following this pattern this in the past?

4. Our holy fear grows proportionally to our comprehension of God's greatness. The more we understand and experience God's greatness, the more we experience holy fear. What steps can you take today to increase your understanding of God's greatness?

CONNECT & DISCUSS

Take time today to connect with a group member and talk about some of the insights from this first session. Use any of these prompts to help guide your discussion.

What is one misperception that you had about the fear of the Lord?

How has practicing the fear of the Lord this week drawn you closer to Him?

What is an area of your life in which you need God's wisdom and knowledge?

What are some of the ways that you want to mature in your relationship with God?

What is something you uncovered this week that made you feel convicted?

What else do you hope to gain as you go through this study?

CATCH UP & READ AHEAD

Use this time to go back and complete any of the study and reflection questions from previous days that you weren't able to finish. Make a note below of any revelations you've had and reflect on any growth or personal insights you've gained.

Read chapters 8–14 in *The Awe of God* before the next group session. Use the space below to make note of anything that stands out to you or encourages you.

WEEK 2

BEFORE GROUP MEETING	Read chapters 8–14 in *The Awe of God* Read the Welcome section (page 23)
GROUP MEETING	Discuss the Connect questions Watch the video teaching for session 2 Discuss the questions that follow as a group Do the closing exercise and pray (pages 23–28)
STUDY 1	Complete the personal study (pages 30–32)
STUDY 2	Complete the personal study (pages 33–35)
STUDY 3	Complete the personal study (pages 36–37)
CONNECT & DISCUSS	Connect with someone in your group (page 38)
CATCH UP & READ AHEAD (before week 3 group meeting)	Read chapters 15–21 in *The Awe of God* Complete any unfinished personal studies (page 39)

REVEALED AS WE ARE

By those who come near Me I must be regarded as holy;
and before all the people I must be glorified.

LEVITICUS 10:3 NKJV

We must *fear God* out of love, not *love Him* out of fear.

SAINT FRANCIS DE SALES[7]

Good works begin with *praise, worship,* and *honoring* and *exalting* of God as the temper of one's whole waking *life*.

J. I. PACKER[8]

WELCOME | READ ON YOUR OWN

Children have several natural instincts that guide their behavior. For instance, they naturally mimic the people around them—especially those who are older than them. They also tend to hide when they are doing something they know is wrong. When a child snatches a cookie, he or she might duck behind a curtain or dive beneath a bed to eat it in a place that is "secure."

Even when caught red-handed, young children will often cover their eyes or try to hide their face behind some object and get out of sight. In their undeveloped minds, they believe that if they can't see the other person, the other person can't see them. And if they can't be seen, they must be getting away with the thing they know they're not supposed to be doing.

It can be cute to watch kids act out of such silly assumptions. How can they not under-stand that we can see them? We know what's going on! Yet such thoughts lead to uncomfortable questions. We often behave the same way with God, our heavenly Father. We know God is omniscient and omnipresent—that He knows everything and exists everywhere. Even so, we engage in actions and attitudes we know are contrary to His will. We sin. And we think we are "getting away" with that sin because God is not physically present to see it.

Such a pattern is evidence that we lack holy fear. We lack not only the reverence and respect due to our Creator and Savior but also the genuine trepidation we should feel in the presence of a righteous God who has told us that sin always carries consequences.

CONNECT | 15 MINUTES

Take a few minutes to get better acquainted with fellow members. Then choose one of the following questions to discuss as a group:

- What comes to mind when you think of the word *holy*?

  — *or* —

- What are some of the ways people project a false image of themselves?

WATCH | 25 MINUTES

Now watch the video for this session. Below is an outline of the key points covered during the teaching. Record any key concepts that stand out to you.

OUTLINE

I. God's dwelling place on earth after the Exodus was the tabernacle (see Exodus 29:44-24).
  A. Nadab and Abihu, two sons of Aaron, offered "profane fire" (see Leviticus 10:1).
  B. Both men perished as a result of their actions (see Leviticus 10:2).
  C. We are wise to heed the *should-be*s and fools to ignore the *must-be*s.

II. You will never find God in an atmosphere where He is not held in the utmost respect.
  A. "God is greatly to be feared in the assembly of the saints" (Psalm 89:7 NKJV).
  B. "I will dwell in them and walk among them" (2 Corinthians 6:16 NKJV).
  C. Ananias and Sapphira offer a parallel encounter to Nadab and Abihu (see Acts 5).

III. Holy fear grows as we increase our comprehension of God's glory and greatness.
  A. The inverse is also true: the less we fear God, the more we will dumb Him down.
  B. Some people believe that God can't see what they are doing (see Ezekiel 9:9).
  C. Ananias and Sapphira thought they could hide their deception from God.

IV. Every human being has three images.
  A. Our perceived image—the way other people perceive us.
  B. Our projected image—the way we present ourselves to others.
  C. Our actual image—who we really are.

V. At the end of history, each one of us will be revealed as we are.
  A. Our secret thoughts and motives will be made known (see 1 Corinthians 4:5).
  B. We will all stand at the judgment seat of Christ (see 2 Corinthians 5:10).
  C. Holy fear helps us to keep our motives and intentions in check.
  D. The fear of the Lord helps us lean into our actual image rather than our projected image.

NOTES

DISCUSS | 35 MINUTES

Take time to discuss what you just watched by answering the following questions.

1. Disrespect is a common occurrence in our culture. When do you remember being disrespected in a way that stands out? How did you respond in that moment?

2. Unfortunately, disrespecting God is also a common occurrence in our culture. Review the story of Nadab and Abihu found in Leviticus 10:1–5. What mistake did they make when it came to showing the proper respect of God? Why were they judged so severely?

3. A similar story is found in the New Testament. Review the story of Ananias and Sapphira in Acts 4:36–5:11. In the church today, what are some ways that we value the *appearance* of righteousness or spirituality more than the truth of those concepts?

4. The more we understand God's glory and greatness, the more we will experience holy fear. What steps can you start to take to expose yourself to God's glory and greatness?

5. Read 2 Corinthians 5:10–11. Paul states that our thoughts and motives will be revealed at the judgment seat of Christ. And that who we really are will be laid bare before God and others. Why is this a *good* thing for believers rather than something shameful or scary?

RESPOND | 10 MINUTES

The book of Genesis relates the fall of humanity occurred as a result of Adam and Eve's decision to reject God's command and choose their own way. Take a few minutes on your own to read this story of disobedience and answer the questions that follow.

> [8] And they heard the sound of the LORD God walking in the garden in the cool of the day, and Adam and his wife hid themselves from the presence of the LORD God among the trees of the garden.
>
> [9] Then the LORD God called to Adam and said to him, "Where are you?"
>
> [10] So he said, "I heard Your voice in the garden, and I was afraid because I was naked; and I hid myself."
>
> [11] And He said, "Who told you that you were naked? Have you eaten from the tree of which I commanded you that you should not eat?"
>
> [12] Then the man said, "The woman whom You gave to be with me, she gave me of the tree, and I ate."
>
> [13] And the LORD God said to the woman, "What is this you have done?"
>
> The woman said, "The serpent deceived me, and I ate."
>
> GENESIS 3:8–13 NKJV

Focus on the questions that God asked Adam and Eve. What can you learn about God from this conversation? What can you learn about the fear of God?

This passage records the first instance of people trying to hide their sin from an all-knowing God. What are some of the ways that people try to hide their actions and attitudes from God today?

PRAY | 10 MINUTES

End your time by praying together. Ask the Holy Spirit to convict you of any ways you have tried to hide your sins from God, and pray you would continue to better understand His holiness so you can grow in your experience of holy fear. Finally, ask if anyone has prayer requests to share, and then write those requests in the space below so you and your group members can continue to pray about them in the week ahead.

Name	Request

PERSONAL STUDY

In the previous session, you explored God's awesome and glorious nature. He is far above anything that human beings can experience or even imagine. For that reason, the more you encounter God, the more you will rightly and appropriately fear Him. In this session, you have been taking a deeper look at the contrast between yourself and God. In a culture that values pretense above reality, the truth that God knows who you really are—and will reveal who you really are—also helps you grow in holy fear. As you work through the exercises in this week's personal study, be sure to again write down your responses to the questions, as you will be given a few minutes to share your insights at the start of the next group discussion (if you are doing this study with others). If you are reading *The Awe of God* alongside this study, first review chapters 8–14 of the book before completing the pages that follow.

THE FATAL COLLISION

Here's an incredible statement: *God dwells in the midst of His people*. This is something we often hear in church, but how often do we take a step back and meditate on that astonishing reality? God, the Creator of the universe, manifests Himself among His creation. He is incomparably glorious, and yet He stoops to join us in our midst.

But there is something we need to understand about God's presence: not every manifestation is the same. We can experience different magnitudes of God's presence. In other words, there will be times when God will blaze forth among us in power, but there will be other times when His presence will be more "dimmed" or "shaded" from our view. Understanding this principle is important for two reasons.

First, when we express irreverence toward God, we will always encounter consequences. But those consequences will be more immediate when God's presence is manifested strongly. Such was the case with Nadab and Abihu and Ananias and Sapphira. They disrespected God in close proximity to His glory, and they lost their lives because of it.

Second, showing irreverence toward God during a time when His presence is dimmed does not mean we escape consequences—it just means those consequences are delayed. This can actually be more dangerous if we settle into a habit or lifestyle of irreverence toward God.

1. Nadab and Abihu "offered profane fire before the LORD" (Leviticus 10:1 NKJV) The word *profane* means "to treat something sacred with irreverence." Where do you see examples in our culture of people speaking or acting profanely toward God?

2. Think back on your actions and attitudes the past couple weeks. Where have you been in danger of treating God in a way that is disrespectful or overly casual?

Hundreds of years after the incident with Aaron's two sons, another set of sons, also priests, named Hophni and Phinehas, were committing adultery with the women who assembled at the door of the same tabernacle. This would be less than ninety feet from where Aaron's sons died on the spot! If that wasn't enough, they were also intimidating the worshippers by forcefully taking offerings. They were "scoundrels who had no respect for the LORD or for their duties as priests" (1 Samuel 2:12–13 NLT). God said of these men, "I have vowed that the sins of Eli and his sons will never be forgiven" (1 Samuel 3:14 NLT). You never want to hear these words from the mouth of Almighty God!

Their behavior was extremely offensive to God, several degrees more irreverent than Aaron's sons, yet these men did not instantly die at the same tabernacle. Why? The answer is found in these words: "The word of the LORD was rare in those days; there was no widespread revelation" (1 Samuel 3:1 NKJV). The lack of God's revealed Word speaks to the absence of His presence; it was nonexistent. . . . However, in the days of Moses it was fully present.[9]

3. God's presence is similarly sparse in many Western cultures today. How should that reality impact our actions and attitudes when it comes to fearing God?

In Acts 2, when the Spirit of God initially manifested on the day of Pentecost, some of those who stood by observing concluded the disciples were drunk on wine at nine o'clock in the morning. Stop and ponder how an inebriated person behaves. It isn't quiet and reserved, rather most often it's a lot of laughter and joy. This describes the atmosphere on that notable day. Our loving God's presence was refreshing and delightful. But when His awesome, even terrifying, presence manifested for judgment in the midst of the same people, the church was gripped with great fear and awe. This event dramatically increased their awareness of God's holiness.[10]

4. When have you experienced the reality of God's justice and judgment? How did that moment impact your spiritual life?

23 Again the word of the LORD came to me: 24 "Son of man, say to the land, 'You are a land that has not been cleansed or rained on in the day of wrath.' 25 There is a conspiracy of her princes within her like a roaring lion tearing its prey; they devour people, take treasures and precious things and make many widows within her. 26 Her priests do violence to my law and profane my holy things; they do not distinguish between the holy and the common; they teach that there is no difference between the unclean and the clean; and they shut their eyes to the keeping of my Sabbaths, so that I am profaned among them. 27 Her officials within her are like wolves tearing their prey; they shed blood and kill people to make unjust gain. 28 Her prophets whitewash these deeds for them by false visions and lying divinations. They say, 'This is what the Sovereign LORD says'—when the LORD has not spoken. 29 The people of the land practice extortion and commit robbery; they oppress the poor and needy and mistreat the foreigner, denying them justice."

EZEKIEL 22:23-29

5. What are some safeguards we can put into place to prevent ourselves from approaching God in an irreverent or disrespectful way? In other words, how can we protect ourselves against profaning our God, who is a consuming fire?

FEAR AND TREMBLING

"How could that happen?" Have you said that recently? Maybe you said it while cleaning up a mess in your home. Or while watching yet another tragic story on the news. Or maybe you muttered those words in the middle of a traffic jam on your way home.

As believers in Christ, we can't help but ask that question as we read through the mistakes perpetrated by God's people in His Word. How could Adam and Eve eat the forbidden fruit when God walked with them in the Garden of Eden? How could David commit adultery and *murder* after all the ways God had touched his heart? How could the disciple Peter deny Jesus after *everything that* he had experienced in Jesus' presence? How could that happen?

The answer is as simple as it is sad: *the loss of holy fear.* We see plenty of evidence for that reality today. As a people, we repeatedly choose our will over God's will because we value our will more than we value His will—we value our pleasure and our plans more than we value God's pleasure and plans. Worse, we feel comfortable disobeying God's direct commands because we genuinely believe He doesn't see what we do or that He is powerless to enforce those commands in a way that will impact our lives.

The author of Hebrews wrote, "It is a dreadful thing to fall into the hands of the living God" (10:31). But we, in our pride, simply don't believe that to be the case. And so, like Ananias and Sapphira, we choose our way without any fear of the consequences.

1. In the previous session, we saw that the more we become aware of God's glory, the more we will fear Him. But the inverse is also true: the less we are familiar with God's glory, the less we will fear Him. Where do you see evidence today that our culture does not bother with the fear of God?

2. Use the following scales to assess how holy fear impacts your actions and attitudes in the different areas of your life.

To what degree does the fear of God influence what you say and do at home?

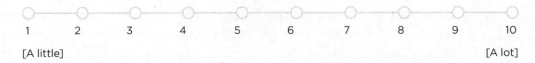

1   2   3   4   5   6   7   8   9   10

[A little]   [A lot]

To what degree does the fear of God influence what you say and do at work?

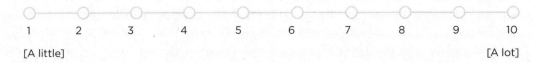

1   2   3   4   5   6   7   8   9   10

[A little]   [A lot]

To what degree does the fear of God influence what you say and do at church?

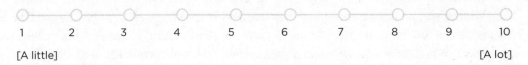

1   2   3   4   5   6   7   8   9   10

[A little]   [A lot]

To what degree does the fear of God influence what you say and do when you are by yourself?

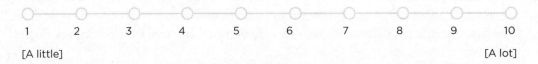

1   2   3   4   5   6   7   8   9   10

[A little]   [A lot]

Let's take it a step further. If someone continues on this slippery path of not just lacking, but shunning, holy fear, they now are threatened with the diabolical belief that *God can't see my motives, words, or actions*. It's one thing to believe God is *not watching*, it is another level of irreverence to think, *He's unable to watch!*

It's possible to hide our words, actions, and motives from other human beings. We can do things in secret—in the dark, even in the shadows—that others won't notice. But when someone believes he or she can hide his or her thoughts or ways from God Almighty, they are self-deceived. This erroneous assumption, whether conscious or unconscious, resides in any soul devoid of holy fear.[11]

3. Dealing with sin, and even sinful habits, is part of spiritual growth. But which of your struggles with sin are specifically connected to the lack of holy fear—to not being serious about God's holiness? Don't be afraid to be specific here.

[Fear and trembling] aren't just words to describe a minor aspect of our life in Christ; rather, they identify how our *salvation is worked out*—a term that describes how our efforts, in cooperation with and empowered by the Holy Spirit, bring to full maturity what Jesus freely provides for us. From this point forward, we'll say it like this: *our salvation is matured through fear and trembling.* . . .

Why isn't holy fear one of the forefront truths taught in our churches, small groups, and Bible schools? Could this be the cause of so many ineffective, lukewarm Christians in the Western world? And could this be the reason Scripture warns in these last days about a great "falling away" from the faith? Paul writes the antichrist cannot be revealed until "the apostasy comes first [unless the predicted great falling away of those who have professed to be Christians has come]" (2 Thessalonians 2:3 AMPC). Could this falling away be fueled by our dumbing-down holy fear? After forty years of prayer, study, and ministry in every state in America and sixty nations, I believe it to be so.[12]

4. Part of working out our salvation with "fear and trembling" means recognizing each day that God is aware not only of our actions but also our thoughts and motives. How can you intentionally increase your awareness that God sees you on that level?

5. The more we fear God, the more we will choose a life that pleases Him rather than focusing on pleasing ourselves. What are some aspects of your life over the past week that have been pleasing to God? How have you sought to glorify Him?

THREE IMAGES

We explored the concept of the "three images" in the group teaching for this week. As a reminder, those three images are: (1) our *perceived image*, which is how other people see us; (2) our *projected image,* which is the image we try to present to others; and (3) our *actual image,* which is what is really true about us.

Our culture is obsessed with *perceived* and *projected* images in a way that was unprecedented even a couple decades ago. This is largely due to technology. It's common for us to spend countless hours and resources attempting to perfect our image on social media sites. We constantly project and present the best parts of their lives—complete with photographic evidence—to a watching world. We make a huge effort to be seen as successful, carefree, and attractive in every way.

The end result is that we can easily lose track of our *actual image*. We can forget or choose to ignore who we really are—who God knows us to be. As we'll see in a moment, doing so is dangerous on many levels.

1. Draw a picture below representing your *projected image*—the way you present yourself to friends, neighbors, coworkers, and others. What parts of your life and personality do you emphasize the most? Include those in your picture.

2. What are the most significant ways your *projected image* clashes or attempts to mask your *actual image*? Where do you feel the most pressure to pretend?

Ananias and Saphira were in a pattern of keeping their *projected* image strong. It all seemed harmless, yet their godly fear was gradually diminishing with every act of hypocrisy. They were no longer convicted of their duplicity. All seemed well and they enjoyed a good reputation, one of which was being the most generous givers in the church. Then the day came when a man named Barnabas brought his offering before the church. The attention of their peers suddenly shifted. They were outdone, and their *projected* image was threatened. Sadly, by this time, the emphasis on their self-made image had already been well developed. The rest is history.[13]

---

3. Review Acts 5:1–11. In verse 11, we read that "great fear came upon all the church and upon all who heard these things" (NKJV). What steps can Christians today take to highlight (and even increase) holy fear within their communities?

---

[9] Therefore we make it our aim, whether present or absent, to be well pleasing to Him. [10] For we must all appear before the judgment seat of Christ, that each one may receive the things done in the body, according to what he has done, whether good or bad. [11] Knowing, therefore, the terror of the Lord, we persuade men; but we are well known to God, and I also trust are well known in your consciences.

2 CORINTHIANS 5:9–11 NKJV

---

4. Paul states that believers *will* experience judgment. We will be revealed as we are *now*, and the way we live *now* will produce consequences for eternity. How would you explain this "terror of the Lord" to a Christian who has never heard about it?

CONNECT & DISCUSS

Take time today to connect with a group member and talk about some of the insights from this first session. Use any of these prompts to help guide your discussion.

What ideas or concepts felt confusing from the material within this session?

What questions from this week's study would you like to have answered?

Think back to that question, "How could this happen?" Specifically, how can we forget that God is aware of everything we think and everything we do?

Where do you see similarities in the stories of Nadab and Abihu and Ananias and Saphira? In what ways do their stories contrast?

What does it mean for a believer to work out their salvation in "fear and trembling"? What does that look like practically?

Where are you in danger of hypocrisy in your life right now?

CATCH UP & READ AHEAD

Use this time to go back and complete any of the study and reflection questions from previous days that you weren't able to finish. Make a note below of any revelations you've had and reflect on any growth or personal insights you've gained.

Read chapters 15–21 in *The Awe of God* before the next group session. Use the space below to make note of anything that stands out to you or encourages you.

WEEK 3

BEFORE GROUP MEETING	Read chapters 15–21 in *The Awe of God* Read the Welcome section (page 43)
GROUP MEETING	Discuss the Connect questions Watch the video teaching for session 3 Discuss the questions that follow as a group Do the closing exercise and pray (pages 43–48)
STUDY 1	Complete the personal study (pages 50–52)
STUDY 2	Complete the personal study (pages 53–55)
STUDY 3	Complete the personal study (pages 56–57)
CONNECT & DISCUSS	Connect with someone in your group (page 58)
CATCH UP & READ AHEAD (before week 4 group meeting)	Read chapters 22–28 in *The Awe of God* Complete any unfinished personal studies (page 59)

IRRESISTIBLE
HOLINESS

In mercy and truth atonement is provided for iniquity;
and by the fear of the LORD one departs from evil.

PROVERBS 16:6 NKJV

The **carnal person** fears man, not God. The *strong Christian fears God*, not man.

JOHN FLAVEL[14]

How little people know who think that *holiness is dull*. When one meets the real thing, it is *irresistible.*

C.S. LEWIS[15]

WELCOME | READ ON YOUR OWN

One of the more shocking moments in Olympic history took place in Turin, Italy, during the 2006 Winter Games. Lindsey Jacobellis was a competitor for the women's snowboard cross event—a downhill race in which contenders make the same run together. Jacobellis took the lead early, but as she closed in on the finish line, she attempted a mid-air trick while navigating a jump. Unfortunately, she ended up skidding on her back. She was only down a few seconds, but it was long enough for the second-place racer to shoot in front of her and claim the victory.

Jacobellis celebrated too early, and it cost her a gold medal. But that's not the end of her story. She continued to compete—at the Olympic Games in 2010, 2014, and 2018—but failed to win a medal. Finally, she competed in the same snowboard cross event at the Beijing Olympics in 2022. At the age of thirty-six, she finally won gold—the oldest American woman ever to win the gold medal in the history of the Winter Olympics.

Lindsey's story illustrates the power of longevity. She did not finish well in 2006. She did not finish the race to the best of her ability. But she *did* finish well in terms of her career. In fact, she is now the most decorated female snowboard cross athlete in history. Why? Because she kept going. She stayed strong for the long haul. Longevity will be a key theme in this session as we continue to study the awe of God. Specifically, we will see how the practice of holy fear will help keep us in the race and position us to finish well as followers of Christ.

CONNECT | 15 MINUTES

Get the session started by choosing one of the following questions to discuss together as a group:

- When have you been able to finish something difficult in a way that made you feel proud of your achievement?

  — *or* —

- What thoughts come to mind when you hear the word *legalism*? What thoughts comes to mind when you hear the word *lawlessness*?

WATCH | 25 MINUTES

Now watch the video for this session. Below is an outline of the key points covered during the teaching. Record any key concepts that stand out to you.

OUTLINE

I. It is through the fear of the Lord that one departs from evil (see Proverbs 16:6).
   A. It is not the *love* of God but the *fear* of God that enables us to walk away from sin.
   B. Millions of Christians are in danger because they *love* Jesus but do not *fear* God.

II. There are two ditches that line the narrow road leading to salvation.
   A. The first ditch is legalism, which ignores the love of God.
   B. The second ditch is lawlessness, which ignores the fear of God.
   C. As a church, we have moved away from the first ditch and fallen into the second.

III. Holy fear is critical for finishing well as a disciple of Jesus.
   A. It's not how we start the race that counts but how we finish it.
   B. Christianity is not a sprint but an endurance run.
   C. The spirit of the fear of the Lord is one of the manifestations of the Holy Spirit.
   D. The fear of the Lord is clean and endures forever (see Psalm 19:9).

IV. Holiness is misunderstood by so many people today.
   A. Holiness means belonging completely to God. It is being set apart for God.
   B. Holiness is cleansing ourselves from all filthiness of the flesh and spirit (see 2 Corinthians 7:1).
   C. We mature our salvation through the fear of the Lord (see Philippians 2:12).
   D. Holiness is not an end to itself but is a doorway into deeper intimacy with God.

V. The difference between positional holiness and behavioral holiness.
   A. *Positional* holiness applies to our status as saved members of God's kingdom.
   B. Our position in God's kingdom does not change from year to year or decade to decade.
   C. *Behavioral* holiness applies to the way we live out our status—our actions and attitudes.
   D. Our actions can—and should—change as we grow and are sanctified.

NOTES

DISCUSS | 35 MINUTES

Take time to discuss what you just watched by answering the following questions.

1. In this week's teaching, you heard about a former pastor who ended up in federal prison. He claimed that he *loved* Jesus but that he did not *fear* God. How do you respond to that claim?

2. Legalism is one of the ditches we can fall into as we walk the narrow road of salvation. What examples of legalism have you witnessed during your time as a follower of Christ?

3. Lawlessness is the other ditch that we can fall into as we walk the road of salvation. What are the dangers of falling into lawlessness—both for individuals and for the church?

4. Holiness simply means being "set apart." Those who are holy are set apart exclusively for God's kingdom and belong completely to Him. In your experience, what does holiness look like in everyday life? How can you recognize that reality in others and in yourself?

5. It is important to remember that the goal of fearing God—just like the goal of holiness—is not to gain "spiritual points" but to develop a deeper intimacy with Christ. What are some ways you have experienced that intimacy, that connection, in recent months?

RESPOND | 10 MINUTES

It's easy to confuse *positional* holiness with *behavioral* holiness. When we accept God's gift of salvation, the Lord declares our *position* before Him to be holy because of what Jesus did for us on the cross. However, he wants our *behavior* to change so that we will mature in our faith and become more like Christ. Take a few minutes to reflect on what Peter said about this:

> [13] Therefore, with minds that are alert and fully sober, set your hope on the grace to be brought to you when Jesus Christ is revealed at his coming. [14] As obedient children, do not conform to the evil desires you had when you lived in ignorance. [15] But just as he who called you is holy, so be holy in all you do; [16] for it is written: "Be holy, because I am holy."
>
> 1 PETER 1:13–16

Peter described Christians as "obedient children" of God. In what ways is following God similar to a parent/child relationship? In what ways is it different?

When you look back on your life, where do you see meaningful progress on your journey toward holiness? Where is God calling you to step more into behavioral holiness?

PRAY | 10 MINUTES

End your time by praying together as a group. Express your desire to move away from any impurity and irreverence that has defined your relationship with God. Ask the Holy Spirit to guide you toward a greater experience of God's greatness so you can increase the impact of holy fear in your life. Ask if anyone has prayer requests, and write those requests in the space below so you and your group members can continue to pray about them in the week ahead.

Name   Request

PERSONAL STUDY

In the previous session, you explored how "the fear of the Lord" will keep your worst impulses in check by reminding you that God will ultimately judge all people at the end of the age. You will be revealed as you truly are—therefore, you benefit greatly by choosing to grow in holy fear *now*. In this session, you explore how the Christian life is not a sprint but an endurance run. A spiritual marathon. For that reason, you need to know what it means to grow in holiness so that you can finish the race well. As you work through the exercises in this week's personal study, be sure to again write down your responses to the questions, as you will be given a few minutes to share your insights at the start of the next group discussion (if you are doing this study with others). If you are reading *The Awe of God* alongside this study, first review chapters 15–21 of the book before completing the pages that follow.

THE FEAR OF MAN

Most of us have not experienced persecution for our religious beliefs. We have not had to face the genuine threat of violence, loss of livelihood, or even death because of our beliefs. This is not to imply that such persecution isn't occurring in our world. There are *many* countries where men and women are facing innumerable hazards for proclaiming the name of Jesus. But most of us living in Western nations have not endured that kind of discrimination or intimidation.

We should be thankful for this! Freedom is a gift we should cherish. Still, Jesus promised that all of His followers would experience trouble. As He said to His disciples, "I have told you all this so that you may have peace in me. Here on earth you will have many trials and sorrows. But take heart, because I have overcome the world" (John 16:33 NLT). To be a friend of God is to live as an enemy of the world, and the world does not let us off easy.

Often, the consequences of rejecting the world's system are subtle—being excluded or mocked, feeling minimized, or having others regard us as "one of those people." Other times, the consequences are more direct. Regardless, as followers of Jesus, we will, at times, be tempted to base our actions on the *fear of people* rather than in the *fear of God*. But we must resist those temptations and instead "work at living a holy life" (Hebrews 12:14 NLT).

1. Think back over your spiritual journey. When has your desire to follow Jesus created a clash or tension with the world around you? Be as specific as possible.

> Paul walked in a high level of holy fear; remember, he is the one who scribed, "work out your own salvation with fear and trembling" (Philippians 2:12 NKJV). He stayed focused on his *actual* image—the one that will be revealed at the judgment—not his *projected* image. This kept him in the place of true holiness and obedience to Christ, even when met with the disappointment, disapproval, or rejection of others.

We should keep this truth before us at all times: *you will serve who you fear!* If you fear God, you'll obey God. If you fear man, you'll ultimately obey man's desires. Often we worry more about offending the person before us rather than the One we don't physically see, especially if we desire this person's love or friendship. For this reason, we are told, "Fearing people is a dangerous trap" (Proverbs 29:25 NLT)—a trap Ananias and Sapphira certainly fell into.[16]

2. The principle highlighted above is worth repeating: *you will serve who you fear!* Where do you see that principle in action in your culture or community?

3. All of us have moments where we must choose between taking a stand for God or shrinking back into a place of conformity in our culture. When was the last time you faced such a moment—the last time you had an opportunity to take a stand for God? What happened?

It is most wise to pursue [God's] Word in our inward parts—the place that governs our motives and intentions. When we view God's Word as the greatest treasure to be found, and obey what's revealed, we enter into the *safety zone.* When we earnestly seek to know His ways as if there is no superior reward, then we know and understand the fear of the Lord and avoid the deception of *projecting* a false image. We are now empowered to live by integrity and truth and have securely planted our feet on the highway (*pathway*) of holiness.[17]

4. King Solomon wrote that if you "search for [Scripture] as for hidden treasure; then you will understand the fear of the LORD" (Proverbs 2:4–5). What are some "gems" you have mined from the Bible that have made a direct impact on your life?

5. Where do you see evidence in your life that you are being motivated by the fear of God? Where do you see evidence that you are being motivated by the fear of people? Use the two columns below to record your answers.

Fear of God	Fear of people

CLEANSE OURSELVES

Longevity isn't a frequent topic of conversation in the church—but it should be. Specifically, we need to be talking about what is required for followers of Jesus to remain faithful not just for a day, and not just for a season, but for decades. Or, better yet, was is required for followers of Christ to remain faithful for a *lifetime*.

Unfortunately, the primary time that we think about longevity in our spiritual lives is when a popular Christian fails or falls in a public way. We read about it in the news, or we hear about it from a friend, we think, *That's such a shame.* It is a shame. But the phenomenon of having our spiritual witness and effectiveness cut short is not limited to pastors or public figures. It can happen to any follower of Jesus.

When we lack holy fear, we risk being derailed by all manner of temptations or skewed priorities—and we make it nearly impossible to finish well in our spiritual walk. This is why we need to *cleanse ourselves*. We must embrace the fear of God so we can walk free from the impurities that chained us in the past and threaten to disrupt us in the future.

1. The apostle Paul wrote, "Therefore, having these promises, beloved, let us cleanse ourselves from all filthiness of the flesh and spirit, perfecting holiness in the fear of God" (2 Corinthians 7:1 NKJV). How does the world teach us to get rid of bad habits or immoral behavior? How does this differ from what the Bible teaches?

2. Paul also wrote that followers of Christ must "put on the new man which was created according to God, in true righteousness and holiness" (Ephesians 4:24 NKJV). What does it mean to put on the "new man"? What does this require us to leave behind?

Paul tells us to cleanse ourselves. He doesn't say, "the blood of Jesus will cleanse us." However, let me make this point clear: the blood of Jesus does indeed cleanse us from all sin, however, we get confused when we mix the *work of justification* with the work of *sanctification*.

When we repented and received Jesus Christ as our Lord, our sins were forgiven, and we were washed completely clean. God buried our sins in the sea of forgetfulness. He doesn't remember them! This work is complete, perfect, and cannot be improved upon. We did nothing to merit this amazing reality, it was a gift from God. This is the *work of justification*.

But the very moment we received justification, the *work of sanctification* (holiness) began. This is when what was done on the inside of us is *worked out*; our new nature becomes an outward reality in the way we live. This is precisely what Paul addresses when he writes: "Work out your own salvation with fear and trembling; for it is God who works in you both to will and to do for His good pleasure" (Philippians 2:12–13 NKJV).[18]

3. What has it meant for you to "cleanse yourself" as a follower of Christ? What are some steps you have taken to "work out your own salvation with fear and trembling"?

Recently after a Sunday morning service a man said to me, "I'm a single Christian. I sleep with women because it's impossible to live a celibate life. I stop for a few months, but then return to sleeping with women. But that isn't the main issue of what I'm here to talk about. My main question is, why am I having so many struggles in my business?"

I was in shock. Have our unbalanced messages of grace brought people to the place of believing they will abide in God's presence and blessings while they live in flagrant sin? In a Q&A at a woman's conference a lady asked my wife, "I really love my husband, but he travels a lot, and I keep sleeping with other men. What should I do? Should I tell him?"

These two really believe they are in relationship with Jesus—but is it the Jesus at the right hand of God or is it a *knockoff* Jesus? These examples are only the tip of the iceberg; I've had far too many similar encounters with other individuals. Is the call to live a holy life so muted that all conviction has been silenced? Yet Paul writes, "whoever rejects this teaching is not rejecting a human being, but God, who gives you his Holy Spirit" (1 Thessalonians 4:8 GNT).[19]

4. Consider the question above: *Have our unbalanced messages of grace brought people to the place of believing they will abide in God's presence and blessings while they live in flagrant sin?* What is the danger in believing that you can abide in God's presence and receive His divine blessings without pursuing holiness in your life?

5. The theological terms *positional holiness* and *behavioral holiness* were mentioned in the teaching for this week. How would you define those terms in your own words?

OUR PURSUIT

There are many things our culture pushes us to pursue in the hunt for happiness: money, fame, relationships, power, honor, influence, purpose, fulfillment. We could go on and on listing what our world believes to be worth chasing. But here is a different suggestion—one that is backed by Scripture and supported by the stirring history of the church. What if we pursued *holiness*?

This is the theme we've been exploring throughout this week's personal study. The fear of the Lord doesn't drive us away from God. Instead, it pulls us toward Him. We are drawn to His glory and greatness and want to know Him more. As we grow closer in our relationship to God, the more we are transformed into His image. We become *holy*.

So, what does it look like to pursue holiness? What does it mean, on a practical level, for us to work out our salvation with fear and trembling? What is required on our part?

1. Think of the people who have modelled spiritual maturity for you—women and men who demonstrated a transformational relationship with Christ. What are some ways those individuals pursue holiness? What do they *do* in order to grow closer to God?

It's worth repeating: *no behavioral holiness, no seeing the Lord*. Why is this so critical?

First, if we don't see Him—if we lack His manifest presence—we can't know Him intimately. We can only know *about* Him, not unlike my relationship with United States presidents. Or worse, we deceive ourselves by creating a fictional Jesus. This illusion is most dangerous because we believe we know Someone we don't. James tells us, "But don't just listen to God's word. You must do what it says. Otherwise, you are only fooling yourselves" (James 1:22 NLT). One who is fooled believes they know someone or something, but in reality, they don't.

The second reason is equally important. Without beholding Him—not being in His presence—we cannot be changed or transformed into His likeness. Paul mentions that those who see the Lord "are being transformed into the same image from one degree of glory to another" (2 Corinthians 3:18 ESV). This transformation begins within and subsequently works out to where it is witnessed by others.[20]

2. One of the landmarks of genuine relationships is that they change—they deepen and grow. How has your relationship with God developed over your lifetime? What do you know about Him now that you didn't know when you first started out with Him?

If we look at Paul's command to cleanse ourselves from all filthiness of the flesh and spirit, it is preceded by a statement often overlooked. A few paragraphs before that he writes: "We then, as workers together with Him also plead with you not to receive the grace of God in vain. For He says: 'In an acceptable time . . . I have helped you'" (2 Corinthians 6:1–2 NKJV).

The acceptable time has come; we can live a holy life with His help. Sadly, God's grace has been communicated far below its potential. It's been taught as eternal salvation, forgiveness of sin, freedom from the penalty of sin, and an unmerited gift. While these realities are completely true, what has not been communicated as widely is its empowerment. God speaks to the apostle Paul: "My grace is all you need. My power works best in weakness" (2 Corinthians 12:9 NLT). Simply put, "Paul, what you couldn't do in your own ability, you can do it now by My power, which is called grace."[21]

3. One of the reasons many people fail to grow in holiness—and fail to pursue it—is because they try to do so in their own strength. Where are you currently trying to achieve godliness rather than relying on God's grace to empower you?

CONNECT & DISCUSS

Take time today to connect with a group member and talk about some of the insights from this first session. Use any of these prompts to help guide your discussion.

What ideas or concepts felt confusing from the material within this session?

What questions from this week's study would you like to have answered?

What are some of the primary threats to longevity in our spiritual lives?

In what ways is the pursuit of holiness an individual task? In what ways does pursuing holiness involve community and the body of Christ?

The pursuit of holiness starts inside, with our hearts. Why do we so often drift to trying to be holy on the outside by changing our behavior?

God's grace empowers our pursuit of holiness. What steps can we take to access or take advantage of that grace? (Kind of like a sail catches the wind to move forward?)

CATCH UP & READ AHEAD

Use this time to go back and complete any of the study and reflection questions from previous days that you weren't able to finish. Make a note below of any revelations you've had and reflect on any growth or personal insights you've gained.

Read chapters 22–28 in *The Awe of God* before the next group session. Use the space below to make note of anything that stands out to you or encourages you.

WEEK 4

BEFORE GROUP MEETING	Read chapters 22-28 in *The Awe of God* Read the Welcome section (page 63)
GROUP MEETING	Discuss the Connect questions Watch the video teaching for session 4 Discuss the questions that follow as a group Do the closing exercise and pray (pages 63–68)
STUDY 1	Complete the personal study (pages 70–72)
STUDY 2	Complete the personal study (pages 73–75)
STUDY 3	Complete the personal study (pages 76–77)
CONNECT & DISCUSS	Connect with someone in your group (page 78)
CATCH UP & READ AHEAD (before week 5 group meeting)	Read chapters 29–35 in *The Awe of God* Complete any unfinished personal studies (page 79)

GOD'S WORD

Your word is a lamp for my feet, a light on my path. I have taken an oath and confirmed it, that I will follow your righteous laws.

PSALM 119:105-106

It is better to *tremble*
at the word of the Lord . . .
than to *shout oneself hoarse*.

CHARLES SPURGEON[22]

The *soul* can do without
everything except *the word of God*.

MARTIN LUTHER[23]

WELCOME | READ ON YOUR OWN

The Vatican Library in Rome is home to one of the most important historical documents in the history of the world: the Codex Vaticanus, the oldest version of the Bible.

Like most ancient documents, the history of the Codex is shrouded in mystery. It was produced sometime during the middle of the fourth century—just a few hundred years after the life, death, resurrection, and ascension of Jesus. The Codex was passed around within the church for a thousand years until it was catalogued at the Vatican in AD 1475, and it has remained in that library ever since.

Actually reading the Codex would prove difficult for most people, as it was written in ancient Greek. But what a sight to behold! The manuscript is comprised of more than 750 pages, or "leaves," and was recorded on a type of parchment called velum.[24]

No matter what version we use, the Bible is a miracle. It is not so much a book as a miniature library—a collection of sixty-six books written by more than forty authors over a period of nearly 2,000 years. We would expect such a collection to be rife with errors and contradictions, but what we find is that the message of Scripture is remarkably consistent from beginning to end.

For all of those reasons and more, we should admire the Bible. But let's not stop there! We should also *fear* God's Word. As the Lord has said, "On this one will I look: On him who is poor and of a contrite spirit, and who trembles at My word" (Isaiah 66:2 NKJV).

CONNECT | 15 MINUTES

Get the session started by choosing one of the following questions to discuss together as a group:

- What comes to mind when you think of "trembling" at God's Word?

  — or —

- Do you have a "life verse"—a passage of Scripture that has a special meaning for this season of your life? If so, what is it?

WATCH | 25 MINUTES

Now watch the video for this session. Below is an outline of the key points covered during the teaching. Record any key concepts that stand out to you.

OUTLINE

I. The person who trembles at God's Word will obey God immediately.
  A. One man whom Jesus asked to follow Him requested to first bury his father (see Luke 9:59).
  B. Another man requested that Jesus first allow him to say goodbye to his family (see Luke 9:61).
  C. When what is not sin takes precedence over the Word of the Lord, it becomes sin.

II. Those who tremble at God's Word obey God even when it doesn't make sense.
  A. What God commands will not always make sense through the lens of our world.
  B. Jesus said that "wisdom is shown . . . by its results" (Matthew 11:19 NLT).
  C. When we choose to obey God, even if it doesn't make sense to us, the results will be amazing.

III. Those who tremble at God's Word obey even when they don't see a personal benefit.
  A. The church in America often attaches obeying God to a personal benefit.
  B. The reality is that obeying God is reward enough.
  C. The story of Esther is a good example of this principle (see Esther 4:16).

IV. Those who tremble at God's Word obey even when it's painful.
  A. Jesus humbled Himself even unto death (see Philippians 2:8).
  B. False religions will seek out suffering in order to please little-*g* gods.
  C. The fear of the Lord allows us to endure suffering as service to God.

V. Those who tremble at God's Word obey God to completion.
  A. Saul's failure to fully obey the Lord God caused him to be disqualified (see 1 Samuel 15:3, 26).
  B. *Almost* complete obedience to God is not obedience to God.
  C. Followers of Jesus have a duty to obey the Lord (see Luke 17:10).

NOTES

DISCUSS | 35 MINUTES

Take time to discuss what you just watched by answering the following questions.

1. Those who fear God's Word obey the Lord *immediately.* When is a time in your life that you failed to act on what God was telling you to do immediately? What happened as a result?

2. Those who fear God's Word obey the Lord *even when it doesn't make sense to them.* When is a time in your life that God asked you to do something that at first didn't make sense to you or to those around you? If you obeyed the Lord in that situation, what benefits did you receive?

3. Those who fear God's Word obey the Lord *even when they don't see a personal benefit in it for them.* Our culture encourages us to ask "what is in it for us" and not act on something if we don't think we will gain a reward. Where do you see the church today trying to make obedience more appealing by making promises or attaching rewards for submitting to Scripture?

4. Those who fear God's Word obey the Lord *even if it's painful.* When has God asked you to do something that you knew would require a sacrifice?

5. Those who fear God's Word obey the Lord to *completion*. In other words, they do not settle for "almost" or "close enough" but choose to obey God all the way. How can you know when you have been faithful in carrying out everything that God has asked you to do?

RESPOND | 10 MINUTES

Perhaps you participated in "sword drills" when you were young. A teacher would call out a passage of Scripture and you would open your Bible and turn to that specific verse as quickly as you could. Of course, these exercises were called "sword drills" because the Bible is "the sword of the Lord." Take a few minutes to reflect on what the author of Hebrews said about this:

> [12] The word of God is living and powerful, and sharper than any two-edged sword, piercing even to the division of soul and spirit, and of joints and marrow, and is a discerner of the thoughts and intents of the heart. [13] And there is no creature hidden from His sight, but all things are naked and open to the eyes of Him to whom we must give account.
>
> HEBREWS 4:12–13 NKJV

What similarities does the author of this passage say the Bible has to a sword?

Read verse 13 out loud. Does that verse feel more like good news or bad news to you? Explain your response.

PRAY | 10 MINUTES

End your time by praying together as a group. Affirm that you will obey God immediately, even when it doesn't make sense, when you don't see a personal benefit, when it is painful, and to completion. Conclude by asking if anyone has prayer requests to share. Write those requests below so that you and your group members can pray about them in the week ahead.

Name   Request

PERSONAL STUDY

As you have seen in this study, the fear of the Lord is connected to His presence. The more you experience God's glory, the more you will develop holy fear. This fear does not cause you to run away from Him but—on the contrary—draws you closer to Him. However, the fear of God is not dependent just on His manifest presence. You can also develop holy fear by exploring God's Word. Indeed, as the Lord said through the prophet Isaiah, "I will bless those who have humble and contrite hearts, who tremble at my word" (66:2 NLT). This is the focus of the personal studies this week—developing a fear of God through His Word. As you complete the exercises in this section, be sure to again write down your responses to the questions, as you will be given a few minutes to share your insights at the start of the next group discussion (if you are doing this study with others). If you are reading *The Awe of God* alongside this study, first review chapters 22-28 of the book before completing the pages that follow.

OBEY IMMEDIATELY

What does it mean to "tremble" at God's Word? At its core, trembling at God's Word means to exalt what it says above everything else in your life. It means elevating what God says far above your own opinions, your own desire, the will of your culture, or even what you might regard as common sense. God's Word comes first.

As we saw in the teaching this week, obedience is the practical response to trembling at God's Word. When we exalt what the Lord says above everything else, we will obey what He says regardless of the cost.

Importantly, there are five distinct aspects of fearing God's Word when it comes to our practical lives. When we tremble at God's Word, we will:

- Obey God immediately.
- Obey God even when doing so doesn't make sense.
- Obey God even when doing so doesn't produce a benefit for us.
- Obey God even when it is painful.
- Obey God all the way to completion.

We will dig more deeply into several of these aspects over the next few pages, starting with the first two on the list: obeying God *immediately* and *even when it doesn't make sense.* As you will see, the Bible is filled with moments when God commanded His people to take immediate actions that did not always line up with the conventional wisdom of the day.

1. Read Matthew 9:9 and Luke 9:57–62. What is the difference between the way Matthew responded to Jesus' call as compared to the way the two men in Luke's account responded? What was Jesus saying about the two men's priorities?

I could continue for the rest of the chapter, and possibly the entire book, sharing commands that don't make sense in Scripture, but based on the results, every one of them proved to be the wisdom of God. Those involved either trembled at God's instructions, obeyed, and were blessed; or they lacked godly fear in their neglect or disobedience and suffered the consequences. I hope you are seeing with more clarity how the fear of the Lord truly is the beginning of wisdom (see Psalm 111:10).

We are told: "Trust in the LORD with all your heart; *do not depend* on your own understanding. Seek his will in all you do, and he will show you which path to take" (Proverbs 3:5–6 NLT). The Lord's wisdom far exceeds our own; therefore, we shouldn't depend on our own understanding. We can easily be swayed from obedience that will ultimately benefit when we are instructed to do something that's not logical. The person who fears God obeys, even when it doesn't make sense.[25]

2. The Bible is filled with moments when God commanded His people to take actions that did not align with the conventional wisdom of the day. For example, having the Israelites march around the walls of Jericho rather than attack the city (see Joshua 6). What are some moments in Scripture that stand out to you as especially confusing or contrary to common sense?

3. We all know on an intellectual level that God is smarter, wiser, and more powerful than we are. Yet, on a practical level, we still struggle with the notion that "we know best." What are some recent decisions or directions you have made that have proven you really *don't* know best?

There are times God will tell us to do something that just doesn't make sense in our minds. But His wisdom is always confirmed by the results. This is why Jesus states, "Wisdom is shown to be right by its results" (Matthew 11:19 NLT).

May we all be like Peter who, after toiling at sea all night with nothing to show for it, heeded Jesus' voice to launch back out to deeper waters and cast his nets once again. That command would take a lot of extra work when they were already exhausted. Don't you love Peter's response: "'We worked hard all last night and didn't catch a thing. But if you say so, I'll let the nets down again'" (Luke 5:5–7 NLT). The results were two boatloads of fish.[26]

4. Peter obeyed Jesus immediately, even though it didn't make sense to him, and the results were a great catch of fish. What are some rewards that you received in your life because of following God instead of what made the most sense to everyone else?

5. Where do you have an opportunity right now to immediately obey God—even though doing so might seem strange by the standards of your culture?

— STUDY 2 —

OBEY WITHOUT A BENEFIT

We mentioned in a previous session that children have a natural instinct to hide when they do something they know is wrong. Another natural instinct often evident in kids is to look for a personal gain in every situation. How many parents have told their children to do something expected—like clean their rooms—only to have their children negotiate some kind of reward out of the deal? "After I clean my room, can I have some extra time playing video games?"

Children are masters at asking the question, "What's in it for me?" But this is a tendency not just restricted to children. Even as adults, we often try to connect *obedience to God's commands* with something that will *produce personal benefits for us*. For example, we know that God commands His people numerous times in Scripture to serve the poor. There are hundreds of verses that give us clear confirmation that God actively wants His followers to care for "the least of these" (see, for example, Matthew 25:40–45). Yet, many times, we will carry out that work not because God told us to, but because we've heard from others that serving will give us a better sense of fulfillment or purpose. It will make us feel good.

This is not acting from a foundation of holy fear. On the contrary, as Jesus said, "When you give to the needy, do not let your left hand know what your right hand is doing" (Matthew 6:3). When we fear God and tremble at His word, we obey the Lord's commands even when doing so provides *no* discernible blessing or benefit in our lives.

1. Take a moment to read through Esther 4:1–16. What was Esther risking by speaking on behalf of her people?

2. Many churches today promote the idea of receiving tangible benefits (including even financial awards) for spiritual acts of obedience. In your experience, what are some rewards you have seen associated with obeying God in the following areas?

Praying on a regular basis	Being a member of a church
Sharing the gospel	Reading God's Word
Worshiping the Lord	Serving others

3. Sometimes a reliance on external benefits can cause you to lose internal motivation. What are some spiritual disciplines that you know you should be doing . . . yet you lack urgency to obey God's will? What might be the source of that lack of urgency?

We live in a fallen world that is contrary, and even hostile, to God's ways. This is why we are informed, "It has been granted on behalf of Christ, not only to believe in Him, but also to suffer for His sake" (Philippians 1:29 NKJV).

Not only Paul, but Peter also writes, "For God called you to do good, even if it means suffering, just as Christ suffered for you. He is your example, and you must follow in his steps. He never sinned, nor deceived anyone. He did not retaliate when he was insulted, nor threaten revenge when he suffered. He left his case in the hands of God, who always judges fairly" (1 Peter 2:21–23 NLT).

We are not to retaliate, but rather, we are to commit any unjust treatment we receive into the hands of God. We shouldn't ignore it, but in prayer we should turn it over to Him. God will avenge us, but in His way and time frame.[27]

4. How do you respond to the statement from the apostle Paul that believers in Christ are "also to suffer for His sake"? What could this look like in your life?

5. What are some of the ways that Peter says we are to follow Jesus' example? What are some areas of your life that you need to commit completely into the hands of God?

OBEY TO COMPLETION

Procrastination is a common problem in our culture. We have a tendency to put things off until later . . . and then we fail to see those things through to completion. But there is another problem that often impacts our obedience to God in more subtle ways. In fact, the problem is so subtle that there isn't a neat-and-tidy word to describe it. The closest word would be *almost*. As in, we *almost* finished. We *almost* succeeded. We *almost* won.

To state this problem another way, many people in our world today are happy to settle for *mostly* completing a task rather than *fully* completing it. As a culture, we have a problem with following through all the way. We are poor when it comes to finishing. When it comes to obeying God, partial obedience just doesn't cut it. *Almost* complete obedience is not obedience. Those who fear God obey Him *all the way* to completion.

1. How would you rate yourself on your inner drive and ability to fully complete what you've been asked to do in the following areas of life?

How dedicated are you at fully finishing the tasks you are assigned at work?

1	2	3	4	5	6	7	8	9	10

[Not dedicated]   [Very dedicated]

How dedicated are you at fully finishing the tasks you are assigned at home?

1	2	3	4	5	6	7	8	9	10

[Not dedicated]   [Very dedicated]

How dedicated are you at fully finishing the little things in your spiritual life—devotions, church attendance, and so on?

1	2	3	4	5	6	7	8	9	10

[Not dedicated]   [Very dedicated]

How dedicated are you at fully finishing the bigger tasks God has specifically assigned for you to handle?

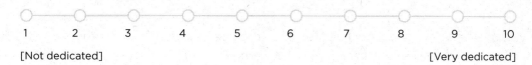

1   2   3   4   5   6   7   8   9   10

[Not dedicated]   [Very dedicated]

2. Take a closer look at the last two questions listed above. In your life specifically, what are the little and big tasks that God has asked you to handle? In other words, what are the specific ways God expects you to obey His Word right now?

When Saul was asked to go to battle, he didn't stomp his foot to the ground and say, "No way! I'm not going to do this!" Most would classify that behavior as rebellion. He didn't ignore the command and busy himself with other personal matters. If that were the case, most would conclude, "He erred in judgment by not making obedience a priority." But few would use the word "rebellion." Likewise, most would affirm he did well by completing 99.99 percent of the assignment, but very few would classify his actions as rebellion. If we were in Saul's shoes and received this correction, how many of us would protest, "Come on, be reasonable! Why are you so focused on the little I didn't do, instead of acknowledging all that I accomplished?" In light of this, it's safe to conclude this truth: *almost complete* obedience isn't obedience at all.[28]

3. Take a moment to read 1 Samuel 15:10–21. Not only did Saul fail to fully complete what God told him to do, but he also tried to justify his disobedience many times. What are some of the excuses Saul used to rationalize his behavior?

4. Settling for *almost* is unacceptable in light of our holy, almighty, all-powerful God. What might be some excuses you are currently using to avoid fully obeying God's will?

CONNECT & DISCUSS

Take time today to connect with a group member and talk about some of the insights from this first session. Use any of these prompts to help guide your discussion.

What ideas or concepts felt confusing from the material within this session?

What questions from this week's study would you like to have answered?

To what degree would you say that you "tremble" at God's word? Explain.

Which of the five characteristics of those who tremble at God's Word seem to be lacking in your life? Which feel like opportunities for growth?

What factors tend to keep you from obeying God immediately?

What factors tend to keep you from obeying God to completion?

CATCH UP & READ AHEAD

Use this time to go back and complete any of the study and reflection questions from previous days that you weren't able to finish. Make a note below of any revelations you've had and reflect on any growth or personal insights you've gained.

Read chapters 36–42 in *The Awe of God* before the next group session. Use the space below to make note of anything that stands out to you or encourages you.

WEEK 5

BEFORE GROUP MEETING	Read chapters 29–35 in *The Awe of God* Read the Welcome section (page 83)
GROUP MEETING	Discuss the Connect questions Watch the video teaching for session 5 Discuss the questions that follow as a group Do the closing exercise and pray (pages 83–88)
STUDY 1	Complete the personal study (pages 90–92)
STUDY 2	Complete the personal study (pages 93–95)
STUDY 3	Complete the personal study (pages 96–97)
CONNECT & DISCUSS	Connect with someone in your group (page 98)
CATCH UP & READ AHEAD (before week 6 group meeting)	Read chapters 36–42 in *The Awe of God* Complete any unfinished personal studies (page 99)

INTIMACY WITH GOD

*The secret of the LORD is with those who fear Him,
and He will show them His covenant.*

PSALM 25:14 NKJV

Faith is the road,
but communion with Jesus *is the well*
from which the *pilgrim* drinks.

CHARLES SPURGEON[29]

It is an *awful condition*
to be satisfied with one's spiritual
attainments . . . God was and is
looking for *hungry, thirsty* people.

SMITH WIGGLESWORTH[30]

WELCOME | READ ON YOUR OWN

Several years ago, a story surfaced about two men who were born and raised in Hawaii. Alan Robinson and Walter Macfarlane met as young children, grew up together, and remained close friends for decades. In fact, Alan and Walter were best friends for *sixty* years. But something happened that changed the nature of their relationship.

Independently, both men began looking into their family histories. Alan knew that he had been adopted, while Walter did not know the identity of his father. So, they began to do some research through a popular DNA-based website. You've probably already guessed what they discovered: they had the same mom! The two men, whose friendship had spanned sixty years, were brothers.[31]

It's quite a story. Deep and meaningful friendship is truly one of the greatest gifts we can receive in life. Incredibly, amazingly, our experiences with friendship are not limited to other people. When we become citizens of God's kingdom and members of His family, we have the opportunity to enjoy a personal relationship with Jesus Christ.

In the opening session, we discussed how a genuine fear of the Lord does not drive us away from God. The fear that we have of the Lord doesn't scare us so that we flee from His presence. Instead, holy fear draws us closer to God. It aligns us with Him and gives us the opportunity to experience true intimacy with the Creator of all things. This is the focus of this week's session—how we can develop that deeper intimacy with God.

CONNECT | 15 MINUTES

Get the session started by choosing one of the following questions to discuss together as a group:

- What traits or characteristics are most important for you when it comes to identifying potential new friends?

— *or* —

- What would you say is most important when it comes to developing deep and intimate friendships with others?

WATCH | 25 MINUTES

Now watch the video for this session. Below is an outline of the key points covered during the teaching. Record any key concepts that stand out to you.

OUTLINE

I. We have the opportunity to establish an intimate friendship with God.
   A. The secret of the Lord is with those who fear Him (see Psalm 24:11).
   B. God does not have the same relationship with every person in the church.
   C. There are different levels of intimacy, and that intimacy is connected to holy fear.

II. Abraham was called a friend of God in the Old Testament .
   A. Abraham proved His fear of God when he was asked to sacrifice Isaac.
   B. Abraham obeyed immediately, even though it didn't make sense, and to completion.
   C. God revealed a facet of His personality to Abraham that no one had known before.

III. Abraham and Lot were both righteous but had different relationships with God.
   A. Both men were "saved." They both were described as "righteous."
   B. God spoke with Abraham about the destruction of Sodom and Gomorrah.
   C. God did not speak with Lot—he was only spared from destruction due to Abraham's prayer.
   D. The difference between the two men was their level of *holy fear.*

IV. Moses was also called a friend of God in the Old Testament.
   A. Moses spoke to God face to face as a man speaks to his friend (see Exodus 33:11).
   B. Israel knew *about* God, but Moses knew Him personally (see Psalm 103:7).
   C. Moses often knew what God was going to do and helped God decide how to do it.

V. Our relationship with God is also based on our level of holy fear.
   A. Jesus did not trust people in general. He knew the frailty of humanity (see John 2:23-24).
   B. Jesus said that His disciples were no longer servants but friends (see John 15:15).
   C. God keeps many of us at the relationship level of servants to protect us.
   D. The fear of God opens up the door to friendship and intimacy with God.

NOTES

DISCUSS | 35 MINUTES

Take time to discuss what you just watched by answering the following questions.

1. People have different definitions of *friendship*. For some, friendship is a casual affair, while for others, it represents a deep commitment to the other person involved in the relationship. How would you describe the way you process the different layers of what it means to be a friend?

2. When Abraham was advanced in years, God instructed him to sacrifice Isaac—the promised son for whom he had waited twenty-years to be born. How did Abraham's response reveal that he understood what it meant to fear the Lord? What did God reveal to Abraham about His nature because of Abraham's holy fear?

3. Both Abraham and Lot were considered righteous, but each experienced a different level of intimacy with God. Abraham knew what God was going to do ahead of time and even helped God decide how to do it. Lot was as clueless of God's plans as the rest of the world. What does the story of the two men reveal about the state of believers today?

4. Moses also had a close connection with God. The Bible says that he would speak with God face to face as one speaks to a friend (see Exodus 33:11). What do you think allowed Moses to have this intimate friendship with God? What are your aspirations when it comes to experiencing this same type of connection with God?

5. Jesus told His disciples, "I no longer call you servants, because a servant does not know his master's business" (John 15:15). This statement implies that at one time, these disciples *were* considered servants. Based on your experiences over the past year, do you feel more like a servant of God or a friend? Explain your answer.

RESPOND | 10 MINUTES

The Bible reveals that we not only can be reconciled in our relationship with God but can also reach the place of relating to Him as a friend. But for us to reach that point, we need to get rid of anything that hinders that friendship. Take a few minutes on your own to read what James says about our friendship with God:

> [1] What causes fights and quarrels among you? Don't they come from your desires that battle within you? [2] You desire but do not have, so you kill. You covet but you cannot get what you want, so you quarrel and fight. You do not have because you do not ask God. 3 When you ask, you do not receive, because you ask with wrong motives, that you may spend what you get on your pleasures. [4] You adulterous people, don't you know that friendship with the world means enmity against God? Therefore, anyone who chooses to be a friend of the world becomes an enemy of God. [5] Or do you think Scripture says without reason that he jealously longs for the spirit he has caused to dwell in us?
>
> JAMES 4:1-5

What do you think it means to be a "friend of the world"?

Think back to your experiences over the past year. What are some ways you have felt pressured to pursue a friendship with the world rather than intimacy with God?

PRAY | 10 MINUTES

End your time by praying together as a group. Declare your desire to live not only as a servant of Christ but also as a friend who knows and is known by the Savior. Commit to taking whatever action is necessary to develop holy fear so that you can experience greater intimacy with God. Finally, ask if anyone has prayer requests to share, and then write those requests in the space below so you and your group members can continue to pray about them in the week ahead.

Name   Request

PERSONAL STUDY

In the previous session, you explored five characteristics of a person who develops the fear of God in relation to His Word. Those five characteristics are perfectly illustrated in Abraham's reaction to God's command to sacrifice Isaac, his only son, as an act of obedience. Abraham obeyed God *immediately,* obeyed even though the command did not make *sense,* obeyed even though he could see no *personal benefit,* obeyed even though it would cause him pain, and obeyed God *all the way.* Abraham truly feared God, and as a result, he developed an intimate friendship with Him that allowed him to begin to understand God at a heart-to-heart level. This is the focus of the personal studies this week. As you complete the exercises in this week's personal study, be sure to again write down your responses to the questions, as you will be given a few minutes to share your insights at the start of the next group discussion (if you are doing this study with others). If you are reading *The Awe of God* alongside this study, first review chapters 29–35 of the book before completing the pages that follow.

— STUDY 1 —

WHERE INTIMACY BEGINS

Studies reveal that most people today believe in God.[32] While it is true that atheism is on the rise, the percentage of people who completely deny the existence of God remains relatively small. Of course, this number includes people who believe in the existence of a divine being who is different from the One portrayed in the Bible. Yet, sadly, this number also includes many who consider themselves to be followers of Christ but carry misguided ideas about God.

Some of these individuals envision God to be distant from humanity. They believe God created the universe but now stands back to watch it spin without any real emotional attachment to it. Or, sadder still, they envision God to be angry with humanity—One who is filled with thoughts of vengeance and is seeking to smite those who step out of line.

This is why the gospel is so revolutionary! It reveals that God is neither distant nor bloodthirsty. Instead, He has chosen to step near to His creation—and even became one of us. He is close! Even more, He desires to know *each and every individual* within His creation. Friendship with God is only possible because He desires that friendship, and He has made the way for us to know Him and be known by Him.

1. We can learn about intimacy with God by studying our relationships with others. Use the following chart identify your most intimate relationships right now—those in which you know and are deeply known by the other party. Along with the person's name, write down any ways you have been blessed by that relationship.

Person #1:	How you have been blessed by the relationship

Person #2:	How you have been blessed by the relationship
Person #3:	How you have been blessed by the relationship

2. Look at the three relationships you wrote down. What are some ways you contribute to those relationships in order to maintain intimacy with each of those people?

[God] deeply desires to be close with each of us. Yet, allow me to reiterate that true intimacy is spawned from *both* parties knowing each other well, not just one. Just as He searches our innermost thoughts, even so we should passionately seek to create true intimacy. Moses pursues this level of relationship by crying out, "You have told me, 'I know you by name, and I look favorably on you.' If it is true that you look favorably on me, let me know your ways so I may understand you more fully and continue to enjoy your favor" (Exodus 33:12–13 NLT).

God doesn't *know* us as merely a number amid a mass amount of people, He knows us personally, individually, by name. In the above verses, we see that Moses wants this reciprocated; his passionate desire is to go further in his knowledge of God. He wants a relationship of intimacy—not only God deeply knowing him, but also Moses deeply knowing God. So what about you and me? We are told, "Come close to God, and God will come close to you" (James 4:8 NLT).[33]

3. Growing in intimacy with God must go both ways. We must learn about His heart and His desires, even as we accept His knowledge of us. What are some steps you will take this week to better open the lines of communication between yourself and God?

The truth is, we haven't even begun to know God on an intimate level unless we fear Him—it's the starting point. If you initiate anything outside of the starting point, you can't complete it. If I begin a 100-meter dash 50 meters ahead of the starting blocks, I'm unable to participate or complete the race. It's no different in our relationship with God—without holy fear, it's impossible to know Him intimately. Thankfully, He has given us a path to know Him intimately, but will we take it? Remember that by the fear of the Lord we depart from evil or *lawlessness*. With this knowledge, consider that Jesus foretells a large group of people who will be shocked on the day of judgment. These men and women call Him their Lord, but are going to hear Jesus say, "'I never knew you; depart from Me, you who practice lawlessness'" (Matthew 7:23 NKJV).... Jesus will say to those who lack holy fear, "I never intimately knew you."[34]

4. The fear of the Lord is the starting place for intimacy with God. We cannot know Him in the way that Abraham and Moses knew Him until we truly fear Him. So, what obstacles are holding you back from developing and cultivating holy fear in your life?

5. What is one step you will take today to search out God's heart and seek to know Him better? Write that step down in the spalce below as a commitment to carry it out before the day is done!

A FALSE VIEW OF GOD

There is a phenomenon in psychology known as the *illusionary truth effect.* The principle basically states that we will believe false information to be correct if we are repeatedly exposed to it. Whenever we are confronted with new information, we assess its validity by comparing it with what we already know to be true. Repetition of the new information makes it seem more familiar to us—and thus we are more likely to be comfortable in accepting it as true.[35]

It is thus possible for us to believe—deeply and passionately—in something that is false. Unfortunately, this can be the case when it comes to our view of God, especially if we have been exposed to misunderstandings about God by our family, fellow Christians, and our church. For example, many well-intentioned followers of Christ believe they can gain access to heaven through a "mathematical formula" of doing more good things than bad things. Others fall into the trap of thinking they can lose God's love and approval by sinning. Many others believe they can develop a personal relationship with God *without* the fear of God.

Each of these beliefs is false. Each is rejected in the pages of God's Word. Yet many people today are marching toward eternity on the shaky hope offered by such fabricated ideas. Sadly, it is possible for us to create a deity with the name of "Jesus" and yet have no knowledge of the actual Christ seated at the right hand of the Father.

1. Read Matthew 7:21–23. Jesus said we can know we are truly serving God—that we are truly connected to Him—when we do "the will of [our] Father who is in heaven" How would you describe what God is calling you to do in this current season of your life?

2. Consider the following false beliefs and then look up the accompanying passage of Scripture. Write down the correct belief according to God's Word.

False belief	God't truth
Doing more good things than bad will secure you a place in heaven	Ephesians 2:8-9
You can lose God' love because of your sin	Romans 8:38-39
You can develop a close relationship with God without holy fear	Psalm 25:14

3. One reason why people build their lives on false beliefs about God is because they fail to critically evaluate their assumptions. What about you? What safeguards do you have to make sure the Jesus you are following is not a creation of your own making?

This discussion is Jesus' closing subject in His famous Sermon on the Mount. To put a cap on His startling words, He concludes with: "Therefore whoever hears these sayings of Mine, *and does them*, I will liken him to a wise man who built his house on the rock: and the rain descended, the floods came, and the winds blew and beat on that house; and it did not fall, for it was founded on the rock. But everyone who hears these sayings of Mine, and *does not do them*, will be like a foolish man who built his house on the sand: and the rain descended, the floods came, and the winds blew and beat on that house; and it fell. And great was its fall" (Matthew 7:24-27 NKJV).

If you examine the two groups, it all comes down to one simple difference. He states both groups hear His Word, but the first group *does them*; the second group *does not do them*—or we could say, the first group *trembles at God's Word* (fears God) and the second group *does not tremble at God's Word* (does not fear God). . . .

These two groups are very similar in appearance. The group lacking foundation, their belief in the doctrine of Christianity, fervently calling Him their Lord, and their active Christian service represent how they built their life, their house. The solid foundation group had all the same qualities, except they obeyed His words as if it were their own will. Both houses are made of the same material, the same teachings. They both look identical in worship and service. The difference is the foundation—the unseen. One group privately experiences intimacy with God, the other group does not.[36]

4. Trembling at God's Word prevents us from creating a fictional Jesus because the Word of God reveals truth. It is much harder to create something counterfeit when we are repeatedly exposed to the truth. This being the case, what are some words or phrases that describe your study of God's Word in the past year? In recent weeks?

5. Genuine prayer is another discipline that prevents us from creating a fictional version of Christ. We can know our relationship with Jesus is solid when we speak to Him regularly—*and when we listen for Him to speak to us.* So, what have you heard from God over the past year? How has He been directing you in recent weeks?

FRIENDS OF GOD

Abraham and Moses were singled out in Scripture because they experienced deep intimacy with God. They were labeled as God's *friends*. This reveals that God does not approach human relationships the same—even among what we would call Christians.

Many wonder if this dynamic changed with Jesus—if all Christians now have the same relationship with God. The answer is *no*. There were thousands of people who followed Jesus during His ministry, yet He did not trust them because of what was in their hearts (see John 2:24-25). But at the Last Supper, Jesus initiated a deeper level of intimacy with the eleven men who had proven themselves to be trustworthy. It was to them that He said, "No longer do I call you servants . . . I call you friends" (verse 15).

Don't miss that wonderful news! It is possible to reach a level of intimacy with Christ in which He trusts you and calls you His friend! But attaining that level of intimacy is not automatic. You must grow into such a relationship through holy fear.

1. Trust is a key factor in our intimacy with God. How have you proven yourself to be worthy of God's trust? How do you demonstrate to God that He can rely on you?

Jesus states to all of us: "You are My friends *if* . . . " (John 15:14 NKJV). We sing songs, preach sermons, and speak casually about Jesus being our friend. However, we rarely finish His statement. The word "if" is a condition; it's not automatic, even if we believe in Him. What is the condition of friendship?

"You are My friends *if you do whatever I command you*."

There is the condition: *the fear of the Lord* – trembling at His Word; obeying His commands instantly and to completion, even if it doesn't make sense, you don't see the benefit, or it is painful. Just as Abraham and Moses were welcomed into a relationship of friendship with God Almighty due to their holy awe, it is no different with us now. When the Lord's heart and will are our number one priority, He then can trust us, and will welcome us into a relationship of friendship. What an honor, what a privilege, and how exhilarating to be a friend of the Creator of the Universe.[37]

2. We cannot become saved by doing good works. God's Word makes that clear. So, how can you process Jesus' conditional "if" statement in light of that reality? How is the idea of friendship with Jesus different than salvation?

3. How would you rate your obedience to God's commands in these areas of life?

Sharing the gospel with those who need to hear it:

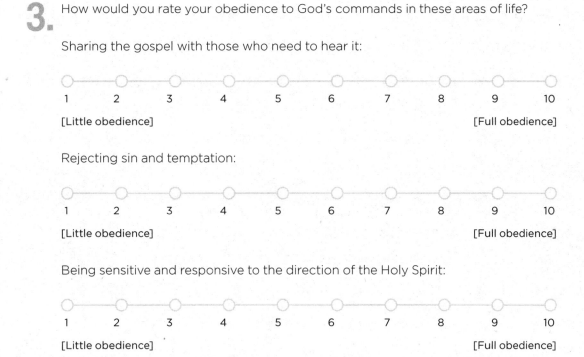

| 1 | 2 | 3 | 4 | 5 | 6 | 7 | 8 | 9 | 10 |

[Little obedience]   [Full obedience]

Rejecting sin and temptation:

| 1 | 2 | 3 | 4 | 5 | 6 | 7 | 8 | 9 | 10 |

[Little obedience]   [Full obedience]

Being sensitive and responsive to the direction of the Holy Spirit:

| 1 | 2 | 3 | 4 | 5 | 6 | 7 | 8 | 9 | 10 |

[Little obedience]   [Full obedience]

4. Friendship with God is a blessing. Intimacy with Christ is a treasure. What are some ways that you have benefited from your relationship with God in recent years?

CONNECT & DISCUSS

Take time today to connect with a group member and talk about some of the insights from this first session. Use any of these prompts to help guide your discussion.

What ideas or concepts felt confusing from the material within this session?

What questions from this week's study would you like to have answered?

True intimacy with God must go both ways—He knows us and we know Him. What does it look like for you to get to know God on a deeper level?

Intimacy with God is stunted when we believe in a fictional version of Jesus. What are some signs that the Jesus you are following is made up or corrupted?

What caused you to feel convicted during the study this week? Why?

How would you describe the connection between holy fear and intimacy with God?

CATCH UP & READ AHEAD

Use this time to go back and complete any of the study and reflection questions from previous days that you weren't able to finish. Make a note below of any revelations you've had and reflect on any growth or personal insights you've gained.

Read chapters 36–42 in *The Awe of God* before the next group session. Use the space below to make note of anything that stands out to you or encourages you.

WEEK 6

BEFORE GROUP MEETING	Read chapters 36–42 in *The Awe of God* Read the Welcome section (page 103)
GROUP MEETING	Discuss the Connect questions Watch the video teaching for session 6 Discuss the questions that follow as a group Do the closing exercise and pray (pages 103–109)
STUDY 1	Complete the personal study (pages 110–112)
STUDY 2	Complete the personal study (pages 113–115)
STUDY 3	Complete the personal study (pages 116–117)
CONNECT & DISCUSS	Connect with someone in your group (page 118)
WRAP IT UP	Complete any unfinished personal studies (page 119) Connect with your group about the next study that you want to go through together

THE TREASURE'S BENEFITS

*Praise the L*ORD*. Blessed are those who fear the L*ORD*, who find great delight in his commands.*

PSALM 112:1

whoever fears God stands above all manner *of fear.*

EPHREM THE SYRIAN[38]

When we are *defining* in what man's true wisdom consists, *the most convenient* word to use is that which distinctly expresses *the fear of God.*

AUGUSTINE OF HIPPO[39]

WELCOME | READ ON YOUR OWN

So, when it comes to the fear of the Lord . . . *what's in it for you*?

Now, we mentioned in a previous session that one of the characteristics of those who tremble at God's Word is that they obey even when they do not see a personal benefit for doing so. We are not demonstrating the fear of God when we respond to His commands by asking, "What's in it for me?"

Still, we need to revisit this idea because we can't walk away from this study with a faulty impression about fearing God. Specifically, we don't want to imply that holy fear carries no benefits for God's people—that fearing God brings us nothing in return.

Far from it! Scripture is packed with God's promises about the rewards we can and *will* receive when we demonstrate holy fear. In fact, we studied one of those benefits in the previous session. The fear of God creates intimacy with God and allows us to relate to Him as a friend. But as they say in cheesy commercials: "Wait . . . there's more!"

Lots more. The fear of God is our natural state—it's what God created us to experience. This means we receive many benefits when we are properly aligned with God in holy fear. Once again, those benefits are not our primary motivation for choosing to fear God and obey Him, but they are nonetheless real. And they are substantial.

So, let's wrap up our study on the awe of God by exploring some of the wonderful blessings we receive when we align with our Creator in holy fear.

CONNECT | 15 MINUTES

Get the session started by choosing one of the following questions to discuss together as a group:

- What have you experienced in the past year that made you shout for joy?

    — *or* —

- When have you received a gift that shocked you? How did you respond?

WATCH | 25 MINUTES

Now watch the video for this session. Below is an outline of the key points covered during the teaching. Record any key concepts that stand out to you.

OUTLINE

I. The person who fears God will have successful children (see Psalm 112:2).
   A. God told Abraham that his descendants would be successful (see Genesis 22:17).
   B. When you have holy fear, you will be blessed throughout eternity.

II. The person who fears God will be wealthy (see Psalm 112:3a).
   A. True wealth is not about material possessions but about influence.
   B. Holy fear gives us the ability (and resources) to influence others for God's kingdom.

III. The person who fears God will have his or her deeds remembered forever (see Psalm 112:3b).

IV. The person who fears God will not be overcome by evil (see Psalm 112:6a).
   A. The promises, blessings, and benefits of God are not automatic.
   B. We have to contend for the blessings of God with faith (see Genesis 25:21).

V. The person who fears God will be long remembered (see Psalm 112:6b).
   A. This refers to generational blessings that occur over a long time.
   B. We remember Jonathan Edwards . . . we don't remember Max Jukes.

VI. The person who fears God will not fear bad news (see Psalm 112:7a).
   A. The fear of the Lord trumps all other earthly fears.
   B. Jesus told us to fear God and not men (see Matthew 10:28).

VII. The person who fears God is confident (see Psalm 112:7b).
   A. When we fear God, we don't have to accept (or choose) discouragement.
   B. When we are confident in God, we can reject complaining.

VIII. The person who fears God is fearless (see Psalm 112:8).

IX. The person who fears God has influence (see Psalm 112:9a).

X. The person who fears God has honor (see Psalm 112:9b).

XI. Those who fear God will acquire wisdom (see Proverbs 4:7–8).
 A. The fear of the Lord is the beginning of wisdom (see Psalm 111:10).
 B. The fear of the Lord protects from the snares of death (see Proverbs 14:27).

NOTES

DISCUSS | 35 MINUTES

Take time to discuss what you just watched by answering the following questions.

1. Imagine someone you didn't know asked, "What benefits have you received from following the Lord?" How would you respond to that person?

2. Take a moment to review the ten benefits of fearing God listed in Psalm 112. Which of those benefits are the most appealing to you? Why?

3. Psalm 112:3 says this about the person who fears God: "Wealth and riches are in their houses." How would you describe the relationship between serving God and prosperity?

4. Psalm 112:7 says this about the person who fears God: "They will have no fear of bad news." How does holy fear enable us to not have to fear bad news? What is the connection between fearing the Lord and trusting Him to watch over us?

5. "The fear of the LORD is the beginning of wisdom" (Psalm 111:10). Why is it important for us to have wisdom? How does God's wisdom protect us (see Proverbs 14:27)?

RESPOND | 10 MINUTES

King Solomon also wrote that "the fear of the LORD is the beginning of knowledge" (Proverbs 1:7). But he didn't stop there—he expanded on that theme throughout Proverbs. Take a few minutes on your own to read the following passage and then answer the questions that follow.

> 1 My son, if you accept my words
>   and store up my commands within you,
>
> 2 turning your ear to wisdom
>   and applying your heart to understanding—
>
> 3 indeed, if you call out for insight
>   and cry aloud for understanding,
>
> 4 and if you look for it as for silver
>   and search for it as for hidden treasure,
>
> 5 then you will understand the fear of the Lord
>   and find the knowledge of God.
>
> 6 For the LORD gives wisdom;
>   from his mouth come knowledge and understanding.
>
> PROVERBS 2:1-6

According to these verses, what do you need to do to "understand the fear of the Lord"?

What has been the most helpful in gaining wisdom over the course of your life?

PRAY | 10 MINUTES

Conclude this session with a time of praise. Specifically, take a few minutes to verbally and vocally praise God for the blessings that He has poured out on your life. Be specific! Afterward, affirm your belief that God will continue to lift you up as you serve Him in holy fear, and thank Him for all that you will receive in the future—including the incomparable gift of eternal life. Conclude by asking if anyone has prayer requests. Write those requests in the space below so that you and your group members can pray about them in the week ahead.

Name   Request

PERSONAL
STUDY

Congratulations! You have reached the final personal study. In the previous session, you began to zero in on the benefits of holy fear in your life. Specifically, you saw how the fear of the Lord opens the door for intimacy and friendship with God, which is an incredible gift. Now, as you conclude this session and this study, you will see a flurry of additional blessings and benefits that you will receive when you live out the awe of God in your everyday life. As you complete the exercises in this final personal study, write down your responses to the questions in the space that has been provided. If you are reading *The Awe of God* alongside this study, first review chapters 36–42 of the book before completing the pages that follow.

THE FEAR THAT ELIMINATES FEARS

As mentioned previously, it is a myth to believe that following God means nothing bad will ever happen to us. Jesus said, "[God] causes his sun to rise on the evil and the good, and sends rain on the righteous and the unrighteous" (Matthew 5:45). Bad things *do* happen to followers of Jesus, and we should expect that to prove true in our lives.

Yet at the same time, the Bible says, "Surely the righteous will never be shaken; they will be remembered forever. They will have no fear of bad news; their hearts are stead-fast, trusting in the LORD" (Psalm 112:6–7). In other words, while we can be certain that bad things will happen to us in this world, we don't have to fear those things.

Jesus said that in the days before His second coming, "On the earth, nations will be in anguish and perplexity at the roaring and tossing of the sea. People will faint from terror, apprehensive of what is coming on the world, for the heavenly bodies will be shaken" (Luke 21:25–26). However, Jesus instructed His followers that when saw these things begin to take place, they were to stand up and lift up their heads, for it meant their redemption was drawing near (see verse 28).

When we fear God, we no longer need to fear negative circumstances. As the psalmist wrote, "Those who know your name trust in you, for you, LORD, have never forsaken those who seek you" (Psalm 9:10). The fear of God trumps all other fears.

1. Anxiety, fear, and doubt have reached epidemic levels in recent years, even within the church. What are some situations causing you to feel afraid right now?

2. God promises many times in Scripture to keep His people safe. How can we navigate the tension between those promises and the reality that we will suffer in this life?

The only time God permits someone who fears Him to go through suffering is if it's granted from above for God's glory. However, even in these situations there is a confidence from holy fear that eliminates human fear. Consider the three young Hebrew men that were brought before the most powerful king on earth, King Nebuchadnezzar of Babylon. He had built a large idol and made a decree that all people should bow before it anytime music was heard in the land.

These three young men feared God and refused to sin by obeying the leader's decree. They were brought before a very angry Nebuchadnezzar, one who could instantly throw them into a furnace of fire. . . . They remained calm and fearless, even though Scripture states, "Nebuchadnezzar was so furious with Shadrach, Meshach, and Abednego that his face became distorted with rage" (Daniel 3:19 NLT).

These men feared God and therefore knew He would deliver them either by life or death. They were hurled into the furnace but came out unharmed, without even the smell of smoke. They remained unafraid, even if it meant death.[40]

3. Shadrach, Meshach, and Abednego traded their fear of Nebuchadnezzar for the fear of God. They had no fear of the furnace because they feared violating God's will. What does their example reveal about what it looks like to demonstrate holy fear?

The apostle Paul, a man who greatly feared God, had the same attitude. When facing possible execution he stated, "I trust that my life will bring honor to Christ, whether I live or die. For to me, living means living for Christ, and dying is even better" (Philippians 1:20–21 NLT). Why is dying to glorify Christ even better or, as other translations say, "far better" than life? The fear of God, which is the beginning of wisdom, enlightens us with the proper perspective on this life and the next. This is why Jesus states, "Don't be afraid of those who want to kill your body; they cannot touch your soul. Fear only God, who can destroy both soul and body in hell" (Matthew 10:28 NLT).[41]

4. Take a moment to pray through the fears you are currently experiencing—or those you have experienced in recent months. What do those fears reveal about parts of your life that you are still trying to own or control?

5. As you continue to talk with God in prayer, identify one step you can take this week to allow the fear of God to trump an earthly fear in your life. Write down what God wants you to do, and then commit in prayer to take that step as quickly as possible.

THE MOST IMPORTANT THING

There are many disquieting trends that take place on the internet today. We don't have the space here to make a list of them. Actually, we probably wouldn't have enough space in this entire study to record the things people do online that make us scratch our head in concern. But there is one practice to mention that relates to this week's study.

This practice is a phenomenon that occurs on internet chat sites where people post problems they are currently encountering and then ask for advice. Mind you—they don't necessarily ask for the advice of people who are *skilled* or *qualified* in the area of their problem. They don't even ask advice from people they know or trust. Instead, these individuals post their problems to the world and ask random strangers to tell them what to do.

What this reveals, among other things, is that our world is suffering a severe shortage of *wisdom*. People genuinely don't know how to respond to difficult or challenging situations. Furthermore, people seemingly have few friends or family members who can give them wise counsel. So, they turn to the "wisdom of the crowd," which, as I'm sure you know if you've spent any time online recently, is not actually wisdom at all. Thankfully, there is a better way for those who choose to pursue the fear of the Lord.

1. How would you define *wisdom* in your own words? What does it mean for a person to be wise according to the Bible's definition?

Wisdom must be discovered; it's hidden, but not out of reach. Once found, it brings tremendous benefits. So how do we find it? "The fear of the Lord is the *beginning* of wisdom" (Psalm 111:10 NKJV).

The Hebrew word for *beginning* is significant. It's found in the first verse of the Bible, "In the *beginning* God created the heavens and earth" [Genesis 1:1]. This word means "the starting place." Holy fear is the *originating point* for wisdom. Picture it like this: consider a storehouse full of all the wisdom you need for enduring success. However, there's only one door and one key that can gain you access: holy fear. Isaiah writes, "A rich store of . . . wisdom and knowledge; the fear of the LORD is *the key* to this treasure" (Isaiah 33:6).

In essence, there is no lasting wisdom outside of the fear of the Lord. Holy fear is the origin of enduring wisdom, but the benefit continues beyond the starting place: "The fear of the LORD is a *fountain* of life, to turn one away from the *snares* of death" (Proverbs 14:27 NKJV).[42]

2. Wisdom can only be found when we choose to fear God. What are some ways you have searched for wisdom in the past? How did you involve God in the process?

3. Do you have wisdom? Use the scales below to rate your own ability to make wise decisions in these specific situations.

How would you score your level of wisdom when it comes to relationships?

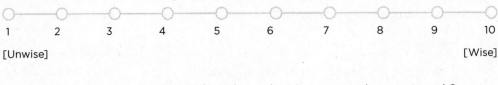

| 1 | 2 | 3 | 4 | 5 | 6 | 7 | 8 | 9 | 10 |

[Unwise]   [Wise]

How would you score your level of wisdom when it comes to issues at work?

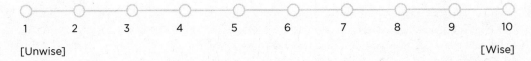

| 1 | 2 | 3 | 4 | 5 | 6 | 7 | 8 | 9 | 10 |

[Unwise]   [Wise]

How would you score your level of wisdom when it comes to your spiritual life?

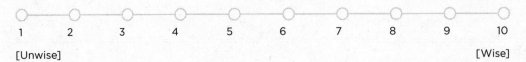

| 1 | 2 | 3 | 4 | 5 | 6 | 7 | 8 | 9 | 10 |

[Unwise]   [Wise]

How would you score your level of wisdom when it comes to finances?

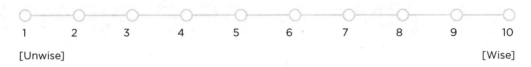

| 1 | 2 | 3 | 4 | 5 | 6 | 7 | 8 | 9 | 10 |

[Unwise]   [Wise]

Presently, in our society, the force of lawlessness is on an accelerated pace. It's as if it's on the upswing of an exponential curve. If the widely accepted counterfeit grace continues to eliminate holy fear from believer's hearts, multitudes of professing Christians will be swept away by lawlessness's deception. We need a revival of holy fear, for it continually protects us from being fooled. It keeps our hearts in line with truth, even when the majority has fallen headlong into deception.

Embrace holy fear as your great treasure. Guard it more diligently than you would millions of dollars, the most expensive jewelry, or the nicest home. We protect these valuables in federally Insured banks, vaults, safes, or by installing alarm systems, yet our greatest treasure is the fear of the Lord. This is why we are told, "Guard your heart above all else, for it determines the course of your life" (Proverbs 4:23 NLT).

4. The challenge is for you to embrace holy fear and guard it as something of priceless value. What are some of the things you most value? What would that look like on a practical level to treat the fear of the Lord in the same way—as a priceless treasure?

5. Holy fear is the beginning of wisdom because it increases your intimacy with God—it gives you greater access to His thoughts and a deeper understanding of His Word. What step can you take right now to fearfully seek out God's wisdom for your life?

A SUMMARY OF BENEFITS

If you've ever had to choose a health insurance plan, you know what a chore it can be. So many forms! So much information! And so little of it designed to be clear, understandable, or helpful.

One of the forms that insurers are required to provide their clients is called a "Summary of Benefits and Coverage." This is a detailed explanation of exactly what will be covered by the health-insurance premium—and what *won't* be covered. Such summaries are filled with information about deductibles, out-of-pocket maximums, and coinsurance percentages.

In this final personal study, you will look at a "summary of benefits" that outlines what you can expect to receive when you walk in the fear of the Lord. Thankfully, the Bible is much clearer than insurance providers on what you will actually receive when you do—and you will find that little is required on your part to receive these benefits! You need only *fear God* above all else.

1. Take another look at Psalm 112:1–10, which describes many of the benefits that you will receive when you build your life on holy fear. Which of the benefits from this psalm seem most appealing to you right now? Why?

2. Confidence is another benefit connected to holy fear. Not confidence in yourself, of course, but confidence that God is with you. What is an area of life in which you currently lack confidence? What makes you feel fearful or uncertain in that area?

In Scripture we are told of Jesus: "The Spirit of the Lord shall rest upon Him, the Spirit of wisdom and understanding, the Spirit of counsel and might, the Spirit of knowledge and the fear of the Lord. His delight is in the fear of the Lord" (Isaiah 11:2–3 NKJV).

There are seven listed ways the Holy Spirit manifests, and Jesus walked in the fullness of them all, but His delight was in holy fear. So the question becomes, how do we receive the *Spirit of the fear of the Lord*? Jesus tells us, "'If you then, being evil, know how to give good gifts to your children, how much more will your heavenly Father give the Holy Spirit to those who ask Him!'" (Luke 11:13 NKJV).

We simply need to ask our Heavenly Father. However, it's not a casual ask, but a cry from our heart and one that refuses to take 'no' for an answer. Just prior to these words He tells us, "Keep on asking, and you will receive what you ask for. Keep on seeking, and you will find" (Luke 11:9 NLT). There's a persistence highlighted here.[43]

3. We have the opportunity each day to ask for God to fill us with "the Spirit of the fear of the Lord." What can you do right now to build that habit into your day? How can you remind yourself to make this critical request on a regular basis?

4. What additional steps can you take in the weeks to come that will increase holy fear in your life? As you consider this question, invite the Holy Spirit to give you guidance and direction. What steps would He like you to take to increase holy fear in your life?

CONNECT & DISCUSS

Take time today to connect with a group member and talk about some of the insights from this first session. Use any of these prompts to help guide your discussion.

What ideas or concepts felt confusing from the material within this session?

What questions from this week's study would you like to have answered?

In this session, you were directed to examine what is currently making you feel afraid in life. What have you learned about yourself by contemplating those fears?

Where do you see opportunities to teach the truth about holy fear in your family?

What have you enjoyed or appreciated most during your study of *The Awe of God?*

What changes do you plan to make in your life based on the material here? How can you help one another continue to treasure holy fear after this study has concluded?

WRAP IT UP

Use this time to go back and complete any of the study and reflection questions from previous days this week that you weren't able to finish. Make note of any revelations you've had and reflect on any growth or personal insights you've gained. Finally, discuss with your group what studies you might want to go through next and when you will plan on meeting together again to study God's Word.

LEADER'S GUIDE

Thank you for your willingness to lead your group through this study! What you have chosen to do is valuable and will make a great difference in the lives of others. The rewards of being a leader are different from those of participating, and we hope that as you lead you will find your own journey with Christ deepened by this experience.

The Awe of God is a six-session Bible study built around video content and small-group interaction. As the group leader, imagine yourself as the host of a party. Your job is to take care of your guests by managing the details so that when your guests arrive, they can focus on one another and on the interaction around the topic for that session.

Your role as the group leader is not to answer all the questions or reteach the content—the video, book, and study guide will do most of that work. Your job is to guide the experience and cultivate your small group into a connected and engaged community. This will make it a place for members to process, question, and reflect—not necessarily receive more instruction.

There are several elements in this leader's guide that will help you as you structure your study and reflection time, so be sure to follow along and take advantage of each one.

BEFORE YOU BEGIN

Before your first meeting, make sure the group members have a copy of this study guide. Alternately, you can hand out the study guides at your first meeting and give the members some time to look over the material and ask any preliminary questions. Also make sure they are aware that they have access to the streaming videos at any time by following the instructions printed on the inside front cover. During your first meeting, ask the members to provide their name, phone number, and email address so you can keep in touch with them.

Generally, the ideal size for a group is eight to ten people, which will ensure that everyone has enough time to participate in discussions. If you have more people, you might want to break up the main group into smaller subgroups. Encourage those who show up at the first meeting to commit to attending the duration of the study, as this will help the group members get to know one another, create stability for the group, and help you know how to best prepare to lead them through the material.

Each of the sessions begins with an opening reflection in the Welcome section. The questions that follow in the Connect section serve as an icebreaker to get the group members thinking about the topic. Some people may want to tell a long story in response to one of these questions, but the goal is to keep the answers brief. Ideally, you want everyone in the group to get a chance to answer, so try to keep the responses to a minute or less. If you have talkative group members, say up front that everyone needs to limit their answer to one minute.

Give the group members a chance to answer, but also tell them to feel free to pass if they wish. With the rest of the study, it's generally not a good idea to have everyone answer every question—a free-flowing discussion is more desirable. But with the opening icebreaker questions, you can go around the circle. Encourage shy people to share, but don't force them.

At your first meeting, let the group members know each session contains a personal study section they can use to continue to engage with the content until the next meeting. While this is optional, it will help them cement the concepts presented during the group study time. Let them know that if they choose to do so, they can watch the video for the next session by accessing the streaming code found on the inside front cover of their studies. Invite them to bring any questions and insights to your next meeting, especially if they had a breakthrough moment or didn't understand something.

PREPARATION FOR EACH SESSION

As the leader, there are a few things you should do to prepare for each meeting:

- **Read through the session.** This will help you become more familiar with the content and know how to structure the discussion times.
- **Decide how the videos will be used.** Determine whether you want the members to watch the videos ahead of time (again, via the streaming access code found on the inside front cover) or together as a group.
- **Decide which questions you want to discuss.** Based on the length of your group discussions, you may not be able to get through all the questions. So look over the questions and choose which ones you definitely want to cover.

- **Be familiar with the questions you want to discuss.** When the group meets, you'll be watching the clock, so make sure you are familiar with the questions that you have selected. In this way, you will ensure that you have the material more deeply in your mind than your group members.
- **Pray for your group.** Pray for your group members and ask God to lead them as they study His Word.

In many cases, there will be no one "right" answer to the question. Answers will vary, especially when the members are being asked to share their personal experiences.

STRUCTURING THE DISCUSSION TIME

You will need to determine how long you want to meet so you can plan your time accordingly. Suggested times for each section have been provided in this study guide, and if you adhere to these times, your group will meet for ninety minutes. If you want to meet for two hours, follow the times given in the right-hand column:

Section	90 Minutes	120 Minutes
CONNECT (discuss one or more of the opening questions for the session)	15 minutes	20 minutes
WATCH (watch the teaching material together and take notes)	20 minutes	20 minutes
DISCUSS (discuss the study questions you selected ahead of time)	35 minutes	50 minutes
RESPOND (write down key takeaways)	10 minutes	15 minutes
PRAY (pray together and dismiss)	10 minutes	15 minutes

As the group leader, it is up to you to keep track of the time and keep things on schedule. You might want to set a timer for each segment so both you and the group members know when your time is up. (There are some good phone apps for timers that play a gentle chime or other pleasant sound instead of a disruptive noise.)

Don't be concerned if the group members are quiet or slow to share. People are often quiet when they are pulling together their ideas, and this might be a new experience for them. Just ask a question and let it hang in the air until someone shares. You can then say, "Thank you. What about others? What came to you when you watched that portion of the teaching?"

GROUP DYNAMICS

Leading a group through *The Awe of God* will be rewarding both to you and your group members. But you still may encounter challenges along the way! Discussions can get off track. Group members may not be sensitive to the needs and ideas of others. Some might worry they will be expected to talk about matters that make them feel awkward. Others may express comments that result in disagreements. To help ease this strain on you and the group, consider the following ground rules:

- When someone raises a question or comment that is off the main topic, suggest that you deal with it another time, or, if you feel led to go in that direction, let the group know you will be spending some time discussing it.

- If someone asks a question that you don't know how to answer, admit it and move on. At your discretion, feel free to invite group members to comment on questions that call for personal experience.

- If you find one or two people are dominating the discussion time, direct a few questions to others in the group. Outside the main group time, ask the more dominating members to help you draw out the quieter ones. Work to make them a part of the solution instead of part of the problem.

- When a disagreement occurs, encourage the group members to process the matter in love. Encourage those on opposite sides to restate what they heard the other side say about the matter, and then invite each side to evaluate if that perception is accurate. Lead the group in examining other Scriptures related to the topic and look for common ground.

When any of these issues arise, encourage your group members to follow these words from Scripture: "Love one another" (John 13:34), "If it is possible, as far as it depends on you, live at peace with everyone" (Romans 12:18), "Whatever is true . . . noble . . .

right . . . if anything is excellent or praiseworthy—think about such things" (Philippians 4:8), and "Be quick to listen, slow to speak and slow to become angry" (James 1:19). This will make your group time more rewarding and beneficial for everyone who attends.

Thank you again for taking the time to lead your group. You are making a difference in your group members' lives and having an impact on their journey as they learn to walk in the fear of the Lord in every situation and circumstance in their lives.

ENDNOTES

1. Oswald Chambers, *My Utmost for His Highest*, January 19, https://utmost.org/quotes/2331/.

2. Charles Spurgeon, "A Sermon Delivered on Sabbath Morning, August 23, 1857," https://www.blueletterbible.org/Comm/spurgeon_charles/sermons/0148.cfm.

3. John Bevere, *The Awe of God* (Nashville, TN: W Publishing, 2023), 15.

4. Bevere, *The Awe of God,* 17.

5. Bevere, *The Awe of God,* 21.

6. Bevere, *The Awe of God,* 34–35.

7. Saint Francis de Sales, quoted in Jean Pierre Camus, *The Spirit of St. Francis de Sales* (New York, P. O'Shea Publisher, 1869).

8. J.I. Packer, *Rediscovering Holiness* (Ventura, CA: Regal, 2009).

9. Bevere, *The Awe of God*, 56.

10. Bevere, *The Awe of God*, 55.

11. Bevere, *The Awe of God*, 60.

12. Bevere, *The Awe of God,* 66.

13. Bevere, *The Awe of God*, 80.

14. John Flavel, *Triumphing Over Sinful Fear* (Grand Rapids, MI: Reformation Heritage Books, 2011).

15. C.S. Lewis, *Letters to an American Lady* (Grand Rapids, MI: William. B. Eerdmans Publishing Company, 1967).

16. Bevere, *The Awe of God*, 94.

17. Bevere, *The Awe of God*, 96–97.

18. Bevere, *The Awe of God*, 118.

19. Bevere, *The Awe of God*, 120.

20. Bevere, *The Awe of God*, 124–125.

21. Bevere, *The Awe of God*, 129–130.

22. Charles Spurgeon, "Obadiah; or, Early Piety Eminent Piety," October 19, 1884, https://www.spurgeon.org/resource-library/sermons/obadiah-or-early-piety-eminent-piety/#flipbook/.

23. Martin Luther, *On Christian Liberty* (Philadelphia, PA: Lutheran Publication Society, 1903).

24. "What Are Codex Sinaiticus and Codex Vaticanus?," GotQuestions.org (updated January 4, 2022), https://www.gotquestions.org/Codex-Sinaiticus-Vaticanus.html.

25. Bevere, *The Awe of God*, 152–153.

26. Bevere, *The Awe of God*, 154.

27. Bevere, *The Awe of God*, 166.

28. Bevere, *The Awe of God*, 171.

29. Charles Spurgeon, cited in "Spurgeon's Morning and Evening," April 1, 2022, https://spurgeonsmorningandevening.com/2022/04/01/morning-april-1st-2022/.

30. Smith Wigglesworth, cited on GoodReads, https://www.goodreads.com/author/quotes/191049.Smith_Wigglesworth.

31. Mary Bowerman, "Two best friends from Hawaii learn they are actually brothers after 60 years," USA Today (December 27, 2017), https://www.usatoday.com/story/news/nation-now/2017/12/27/two-best-friends-hawaii-learn-they-actually-brothers-after-60-years/983673001/.

32. Lydia Saad and Zach Hrynowski, "How Many Americans Believe in God?", Gallup, June 24, 2022, https://news.gallup.com/poll/268205/americans-believe-god.aspx.

33. Bevere, *The Awe of God*, 185.

34. Bevere, *The Awe of God*, 186–187.

35. "Illusory Truth Effect," Wikipedia, https://en.wikipedia.org/wiki/Illusory_truth_effect.

36. Bevere, *The Awe of God*, 198-199.

37. Bevere, *The Awe of God*, 222.

38. St. Ephraim the Syrian, *On the Fear of God and the Last Judgment* (c. AD 306–373), http://www.orthodox.cn/patristics/300sayings_en.htm.

39. Augustine of Hippo, *The Enchiridion* (c. AD 354–430), https://www.logoslibrary.org/augustine/enchiridion/002.html.

40. Bevere, *The Awe of God*, 235–236.

41. Bevere, *The Awe of God*, 236.

42. Bevere, *The Awe of God*, 248.

43. Bevere, *The Awe of God*, 273.

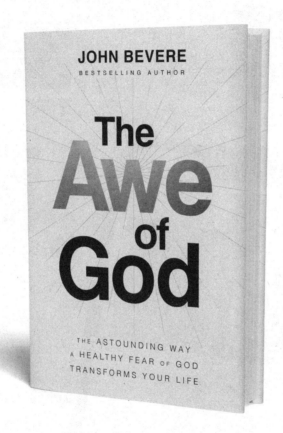

Free Courses, Audiobooks & More to Help You Grow in Your Faith.

The MessengerX app is a revolutionary tool that connects you with world-class teachers, authors, and leaders who will help you embrace a vibrant faith in your everyday life.

Scan the QR code to dowload MessengerX

MessengerX

BOOKS BY JOHN

Messenger International was founded by John and Lisa Bevere in 1990. Since its inception, Messenger International's God-entrusted messages have transformed millions of lives worldwide. Our mission is to develop uncompromising followers of Christ who transform our world.

Call: **1-800-648-1477**

Email: **Mail@MessengerInternational.org**

Visit us online at: **MessengerInternational.org**

Connect with John Bevere:

JohnBevere.com

From the Publisher

GREAT STUDIES

ARE EVEN BETTER WHEN THEY'RE SHARED!

Help others find this study:

- Post a review at your favorite online bookseller.

- Post a picture on a social media account and share why you enjoyed it.

- Send a note to a friend who would also love it—or, better yet, go through it with them!

Thanks for helping others grow their faith!